Meera Ke Muhammad-
Meera's Muhammad

Bhavin Shastri

Become
Shakespeare
.com

First Published in 2022

Becomeshakespeare.com

One Point Six Technologies Pvt Ltd
119-123, 1st Floor, Building J2, B-Wing,
Wadala Truck Terminal, Wadala (East),
Mumbai 400022, Maharashtra, India
T: +91 8080226699

Cover design by D3 Designs

This book is a work of fiction. Any resemblance to persons, living or dead, is purely coincidental.

ISBN - 978-93-5458-942-3

About the Author

A sufi singer, internationally celebrated artist dwelling into voyage of life, spirituality and creativity. A believer in the power of universe. A motivational speaker and spiritual enthusiast.

The priceless heritage of desert - Meera and Muhammad

The legacy they left behind shall remain unmaligned to infinity.

On the one hand, establishment of Islam happened to be religion and responsibility for Muhammad, The Prophet. A responsibility that he sacrificed all his life protecting and nurturing Islam. He did not back down from the sacrifice of his loved ones too.

On the other hand, Meera set up an unscripted religion of love which is a philosophy of accomplishment. Mohan was a witness to her dedication while Meera transcends into the language of love; the voice of love.

On the path of devotement, The Prophet chose deeds and responsibilities, while Meera remained devoted to love. Love that was the only religion, and it still is.

The Holy Quran Sharif, an integration of the Prophet's words, guide us even today, while Meera's life itself is a scripture of love and perseverance.

Wilfulness and persistence in their faith; compassion and sensitivity in actions along with the acceptance of the third one who was not even visible are the common attributes apart from the widespread desert between them.

So, this is the story of a man of sword and awareness, The Prophet, and the irrational Meera who rose from the soil of the desert.

Meera Ke Muhammad
Meera's Muhammad

A book that defines possibilities.

Before we reach to any conclusion just by reading the name, let us know a little about the title.

This book talks about the possibilities that we have routed through love and devotion. Anyone who knows about the life of Gautama Buddha, is aware that it is possible for everyone to become a Buddha. Buddhahood is not about a person. It is the state of being; state of awareness and a state of compassion.

Meera, a famous saint who lived her life searching for herself, drowned in love and devotion is seen in ties with the name 'Krishna'.

However, Meera's devotion was beyond name, form and presence. This devotion was a way of attainment towards self-discovery.

This book talks about the dimension that was left untouched.

Here we talk only of transformation, which is possible for everyone.

The main purpose of this book is to mention about the name that transcends into state, an achievable state for everyone. This is why we are calling it a book of possibility.

Hopefully, we will be able to present a new approach to you.

Index

Unfathomable Truth

'Where does your mercy end?

I see a glimpse of you every moment and find your presence in every creation.

The eyes open in the morning and we find ourselves alive. What else can be a better proof of God's existence? However, it becomes difficult to believe in something that is invisible and we cannot touch it, so is God.

No matter what, whether we believe it or not, the truth is that there is someone who is the creator. A power that establishes balance and control in the whole universe every moment despite being invisible.

This belief in creator draws our attention to the fact that no one teaches the new born to breathe, yet he is able to breathe.

Does anyone teach a fish to swim? Why is a bird born with wings? Every creature is different, everyone's needs and necessities are different, and still the universe caters to all the differences. Every creature has an avenue for survival.

For all different beings, their actions and conduct are different, yet related to each other.

Like a lion's *karma* is hunting a deer and the deer's action response is to save its life and then one day, finally be hunted. That's how the habitation is diversified.

The question arises, despite all differences, how does the whole thing looks so systematic? Who is the captain of this large ship? Is there someone who drives this caravan? Does this thought not rise in us?

Thought!

Yes, the most special thing that we humans are only blessed to have is thought. If we can think, then we have a chance of moving forward. There is scope for search and growth. Otherwise, in absence of thoughts evolution may stop. Although, growth has different meaning and prophesy for different individuals, however, progression is important.

Let's come back to the topic of faith. Faith in the presence of that invisible power, but in its absence too.

Does this presence and absence establish a firm belief in us? What is this belief based on? What is its importance in the life of a human being?

Presence of God is more of emotions that we carry within, yet we consider him to be everywhere. And at the same time, we are aware he is not.

This may sound like a contradiction. However, actually we should have faith in God's presence because it is not there. And when we start believing in his absence, when we agree that it is not there, then maybe it becomes even easier to have faith in HIM.

When the same unfathomable truth appears in both its existence and its absence, then we are prepared to trust ourselves. Now if there is no one, there is no presence of anyone, then it becomes most important to have faith in us, because after all we are there, we the seekers of God. And perhaps this is the only option and solution.

Qualities like truthfulness, non-violence, kindness, compassion, tolerance, and mentorship have been considered as the character of God and we can discover the same characteristics in ourselves.

So, can we see it as a God's conspiracy to make us believe in ourselves? Does not this look like his preparation to tell us that he is there, within us? He is living, breathing, celebrating in us.

Meera knew that there is no other God in any other form. That is why Meera accepted herself as the centre of all energy and devotion and went on her own quest, embracing her Mohan who was again within her. To love Mohan is an example of how Meera wanted to convince herself that there is no such thing in real presence as a form, that you can love. And, when there is none present, you are yourself.

From here begins the faith on absence of the presence and vice-versa.

When this belief reaches its peak, then our own capacity increases so much that no one else remains important, nor required. Then a new journey begins of Meerahood, a state that is completely aware of the non-presence of someone else to love or to worship anywhere outside us. The journey from Muhammad To-Mohan- to ultimately becoming Meera. Evolution of man into consciousness.

Evolution of Muhammad from Meera;

Meera’s Journey to Muhammad.

Meera’s Muhammad

Meera's Muhammad

Did the name startle you?

Amalgamation of Meera in Muhammad. The cosmic merger of two different entities into one soul. The difference is not only in name, religion or culture, the difference that is of time and era. Can we envisage this thought?

Meera, a consciousness and Prophet Muhammad her cognizance to explore the heights.

Muhammad Sahib to be a source of perseverance and patience for Meera.

Something eternal, an everlasting state which was beyond time and beyond space.

Now, can we see the possibilities of little bit of Meera in all and little bit of Muhammad in all that exist? In all of us? And then they come together to make a complete existence.

Can we believe that we are born with the possibilities to reach the highest levels of realization?

We do not realize that we all are part of cosmic consciousness, the way Meera was and in a similar way was Muhammad Sahib.

The self is realized when we become completely integrated,

completely one with this cosmic consciousness, which is what happened to Meera and she found the her own inner self being a source of consciousness, and Mohan was a face of that consciousness for her, a path to discover herself, her own form.

Through the existent to non-existent, the transcendence of human to divine, what Meera could experience, is possible for all.

The way Meera found her own form in Krishna, there is a possibility that she could have found the similar depths of awareness in Muhammad Sahib too. There are no boundaries to cosmic consciousness.

The purpose here is misunderstood, it is never about devoutness to some, it is about searching the self. The source can be any, we may find through ourselves, or any name or path, the ultimate destination of finding self.

Can we conceive the idea that we have Meera and Muhammad both, living with us, within us?

Does that make a difference? Does it make us curious to know what is inside this?

We, consider here that everyone is aware of Meera and Muhammad Sahib, The Prophet. Even if not aware of their complete journey, maybe of bits and pieces.

Would just say that little bit of homework is required before we start this book if are completely unaware of them.

Meera and Muhammad, what is the first thought that comes

to your mind, while reading this?

If you are expecting a religious propaganda, then this book is not for you.

We are not talking about religious differences. Not about diversities to the origin of different religions.

Or, is it us wanting it to be a whoopla of Hinduism vs Islam?

Can we accept Meera and Muhammad together? And may be, Meera's devotion for Muhammad instead of Mohan.

Can it be Meera's Muhammad instead of Meera's Mohan?

Can she be still respected equally if her devoutness flows for Muhammad Sahib instead of Mohan?

Meera's devotion was never about religious bounds and social barriers. It was about a way, a path that she chose to support her spiritual search.

It is about every individual and the different possibilities which we have as humans. It is about the transcendence of a human in divine love.

Are we open to see our beliefs being shaken? The image of Meera that we have in our mind, can we break and can we let Meera find her way on her own? Can we imagine Meera worshipping Muhammad instead of Mohan?

Instead of instilling her with someone, let her decide on her own. Her devotion, love and sensuality may change the direction of their flow. She may re-live the austerities of a hermit she might have practiced then for Mohan; she does the same for Muhammad now.

Or, is it not a possibility that she does not have to go through it for anyone?

All the judgements are not binding only to religion and of course we are not talking of discriminations. Devotion is for liberation, not for bondages.

To reiterate, here we are not talking about religious differences or similarities. We are not going to talk about the philosophies of life and way of living.

This book is about the possibilities that two different souls had in their lifetime. Those who were born in different eras, and walked on the path of spirituality in similar ways. Two existences, who were in force during different times, yet their search was same. Their belief was similar in the non-existent energy that led them to the search of the self. The search of non-existent energy that took them both to the state of complete ecstasy.

The state of complete no-mind. The state where no thoughts and no differences survived. The complete purity. That is what Meera is all about.

Acceptance

What is the true meaning of acceptance? Whatever is there, is all; is it acceptance? Or is that also about understanding the situation and circumstances and then deciding our actions based on them?

What arises now is perfect, either one should accept it or do something to set it right. Even after acceptance if we have a purpose and an eye that can see the need for change, then while walking on the path of acceptance, actions should be such that a purpose is established.

Islam would not have been united and established if Hazrat Muhammad Sahib had accepted the situation but never tried to change it. He accepted the facts and then worked through the way which was required to save mankind from creating more massacres. Knowing one's karmas along with complete reception of situation and circumstances is acceptance in true sense.

In this the real acceptance for him, the Prophet, was the acceptance of results of his actions too.

If everything was dependent only on the acceptance of things in the state they were in, then what was the need of references?

Scriptures like Gita and Quran, they talk about acceptance and surrender undoubtedly but at the same time they also talk of karmas, actions. And, yes, an outlook that does not bound us with the result of those karmas.

But it also needs to be understood that nothing is possible without acceptance? Believe it or not, what is certain, is going to happen only. If it is accepted, then only it is possible to comprehend your actions and to know the need and knock of the time ahead.

Deeds based upon the acceptance of situations, people, emotions, and circumstances are the real actions, *Karma*.

Doubt, fear, sorrow, love, joy, jealousy, and anger are all very natural feelings. No human being can escape from them, neither can we separate ourselves from them.

We cannot reject them by supressing nor ignore them, because these are all the avenues through which we finally get the true meaning of acceptance that leads to compassion and gratitude.

To live life as it comes, maybe in reality this is considered to be the meaning of acceptance. But is it that easy? Can we see life as an offering of prayer? Have we ever felt gratitude for a single breath that we are bestowed with?

We do not even realize importance of breath, yet it is going on non-stop.

Inhaling and exhaling are natural process, we do not even need to accept it. Would it be possible for us to accept other things also as a natural phenomenon? Even our emotions, they are natural too. Hatred or compassion, these are natural feelings. And once they are accepted, then only can we proceed towards liberation.

Have we ever analysed the colour and taste of the sacraments? That's the acceptance.

Whatever it is, it will definitely have some special purpose. This thought helps in acceptance of all other doubts.

Even If we are buried under a mountain of sorrows, then perhaps it will also have some purpose. Maybe hidden underneath are the opportunities for our growth. At the time of panic, finally stirring of thoughts leads to realization, panic becomes an opportunity.

Generally, problems are the ones that have opportunity of expansion hidden in them.

Having said that, when we are in trouble it is also right to accept it as trouble, instead of ignoring. If we have doubts, then that too is also natural. Simply pain is pain and what aches, aches.

By rejecting any emotion in any way, if we try to suppress or hide it, then it will only lead to the intensification of the problem. It is good to accept and face challenges open heartedly than to ignore them and then the chances are to outgrow them.

In this whole event of acceptance, maybe we gradually learn to accept everything else but what takes a lot of time and energy is to accept our own selves. Whatever we are, we do not have to reject it, just be with yourself first to know your hidden potentials. The real process is to wake up. Whatever you do, do it consciously. If you are suffering, you should also face the pain consciously, accept it and live every moment of happiness as celebration.

By acknowledging ourselves, we start on the first step towards acceptance. Then later it opens as a possibility and belief that there must be some purpose in a negative or positive situation. And by the way, what ultimately is the difference between the two?

And this is the biggest reason that we need to recognize our abilities and accept them. And then after this acceptance, the fight for rights can be battled.

We spend our whole life desiring futile things.

The day we get liberation from aspirations, from that day onwards one starts to feel accomplished because from that point the transaction of losing and gaining ends.

Acceptance by itself is difficult as it goes through emotional turbulence. However, acceptance of the self is most difficult. We doubt ourselves the most because whole of our life, we strive to become someone or something else.

But once we conquer the self, we realise that doubt can make acceptance even stronger, and then there is a possibility of something that has never been thought of.

When son of God Jesus was to be crucified, he who devoted

his life spreading the divine message had doubted once even of the God's presence. On the cross he cried and asked "Why have you forsaken me?" At that very moment something happened, maybe a miracle, he realised his disbelief and immediately agreed to God's wish saying "Thy will shall be done". It is said that this moment became the moment of salvation for Jesus and, filled with compassion, he surrendered himself to God.

Mohan too happily accepted whatever came across and yet kept on performing his karmas. Whether it was his journey from Gokul to Mathura. After growing up on the banks of Yamuna, playing flute with his Gwal and Gopi friends, going to fight and win over Kamsa might have looked difficult. Leaving his love Radha and his foster parents behind, a real challenge.

Mohan happily accepted Kubja's love and devotion and liberated her from suffering without any comparison based on her physical conditions.

If you think of Hazrat Muhammad, how would he have faced community opposition? It looks like that he had accepted the protest as well, he was prepared for it. When he perceives an instruction that it was time for him now to spread his knowledge and revelations in the society, he began talking of his experiences. But then community was not in shape of accepting what he said as they had their own conventional beliefs. Certainly, it was not easy to convince masses for something that was beyond their customs. There have been many persecutions against Muhammad Sahib in the initial stages and gradually what started with rejections were accepted by all.

There were attacks and threat to life for Muhammad Sahib but he accepted all. Unprovoked, He kept on moving ahead.

Of course, there must have been trouble, he might have been thinking, for whom is he doing all this?

But he was on duty, serving his God, had to walk.

Actually, the point is that even battles start with acceptance. First acceptance should be of purpose, second of losing the fight, and then on the ability to fight and then establish that the purpose of battle is met.

Khadija who was first wife of the Prophet is known to be the only supporter of Muhammad Sahib when no other believed in him. She was the first person who considered Hazrat Muhammad to be God's prophet and believed his words. On her death he might have been broken, but he must have accepted this loss as well. Although he might have shivered, might have been shaken but he kept on walking his way accepting it all and at the same time performing his duties towards societal changes.

He might have accepted the truth that where there is love, there is oneness. There is only one soul.

What could have been Meera's thought process when she was thinking of Mohan? Did she ever think Mohan would ever accept her or not? Did she ever question herself on devoting her entire life in worshipping Mohan and craving for his one glimpse?

Did Meera ever care about this transaction? There was love, there was devotion, and there was unwavering faith. She had no time to spend on anything else other than loving her Mohan. For Meera to think about the redemption never existed as she had completely accepted Mohan. What difference would it make when Mohan was not there only? There were no two for Meera, so it was not a mess at all. No transactions at all.

Actually, the fact is that if anything is fully accepted, if we adopt any emotion fully, then we are automatically freed from it. Perhaps this is how Meera's liberation from Mohan happened. And for this, she must have first accepted herself.

When no one else exists, we have to accept ourselves for us. Accepting who we are. And the day it is accepted, there will be no scope for anger, expectation and arrogance. When the anger is accepted it becomes celebration.

There is no declaration of acceptance. It cannot be expressed but from the day we accept ourselves, we start growing into witness of all the deeds.

Naturally, there is a long way before we reach to the heights of acceptance. Efficiency, dedication, authority and ultimately exclusion and then after all this, the seeds are sprouted which flower as 'acceptance'. Let us know how all of these, despite being different, become the essence of life.

We are born to be emperors, but we live our whole life begging because we are unaware of our potential. We need to learn to accept our inner questions as well as thoughts. Just be what it is. Meera accepted who she was.

The problem is that we accept only what we feel is favourable. God is also accepted depending upon our choices. He who is omnipresent but invisible, has been given shape, colour and place on our discretion.

Meera is not only difficult, there will be challenges as well. And the biggest challenge is surrender, but to 'whom' is the even bigger question.

Meera was always aware that Mohan was not present, yet she could dedicate herself to him, maybe she could have done the same to Muhammad.

So that is why it is important that when we are trying to understand a book, a thought process, then we should accept it first. Here, we do not mean about the righteousness, but about the thought process. Every thought has a reason.

This acceptance of one thought can establish peace. We can drop all the battles and accept both together -- Mohan's teachings and path laid down by Hazrat Muhammad , will become one.

Ability-Authority-Surrender

Authority is not earned just by asking or fighting for it.

Authority depends on our ability of dedication that leads to surrender.

Are Ability, Authority, and Dedication and Surrender the same? Is there any connection between these words? Are these mere words?

Not sure of their similarity, yes they are connected with each other. Life is combination of all these four. Our capacity to devote the self which leads to submission of the self which allows us the right to belong and own.

Krishna's friend Uddhav once asked him, "Madhava, could you not save Draupadi from the humiliation she had to suffer before the whole congregation, a hall full of people?" Then why didn't you stop this event well in advance? Draupadi was your friend. How could you see her being insulted? Forcibly grabbing by the hair and bringing her to the assembly full of people, yet no one to help her?"

Mohan just smiled and said, "The time was not right."

Uddhav thought, what time could be not right for Mohan? When Uddhav repeatedly asks why was it not the right time earlier to save Draupadi? Then Mohan replies, "Draupadi's arrogance needed to be hurt and broken. Her ego was greater than she herself, therefore she was deprived of the feeling of devotion."

Draupadi acutely lacked dedication. As long as that layer of ego does not break, who can help anyone? Draupadi first fought and quarrelled, then she cursed and expressed anger. Nothing could stop the humiliation and Draupadi kept on struggling to save her honour. She appealed to everyone present in that huge majestic hall for help, but no one could help her.

She broke and wept, but there was no hope. Ultimately, Draupadi gave up all efforts and surrendered herself to the almighty who she felt could have protected her at that time. Now both her ego and anger were broken. Draupadi accepted the situation and refrained from struggling.

Now Draupadi was completely immersed in Mohan's remembrance, peering into her inner self. Mohan was just waiting for that one moment. Draupadi surrendered willingly, and now how Sakha Mohan would not arrive to help?

There are two ways to live life - a way of struggle and a way of surrender. As long as there is struggle, there is a little ego, as long as there is a rebel alive, we are away from surrender.

The struggle that Draupadi had to face because of her ego was never evident in Meera's case. Even in odd circumstances, Meera had accepted the strength of God's will and had left herself to him. Since then, there was no need to fight ever again.

Similarly, it was possible that the war of Mahabharata would have ended without fighting. If Mohan had a wish, but it was not always about desires.

If we think carefully, even when we are in worship or prayer, we are still against his (God's) will, because usually we ask for something that we do not have. This is due to the lack of gratitude and trust in giver.

When the creator and we were united as one, it is really a surrender. The *Sangam* of two in one. Draupadi became completely devoted, because she had surrendered herself. Meera lived this state right from beginning to the end.

Such was her dedication to Mohan, that whatever the situation maybe, resentment, believe, distrust, fight, happiness, love, devotion; she surrendered only to Mohan who was all for her. Mohan was both Husband and God to her. Mohan only was celibacy and celebration.

Meera had found her union in Mohan, the non-existent. What else could be of more importance after that?

There is a great thing to learn from Eagles flying in the sky. We desire for the heights of a bird, but we do not realise its surrender. If we see carefully, when the eagle reaches to a certain altitude, it does not flap its wings. It spreads its wings and glides in the air effortlessly. The same state of naturalness comes to our consciousness, when we surrender. Then we do not flap wings, we trust the wind and its flow. We flow with it without fear. That very moment we discard our burdens and we become *absolutely liberated.*

The load arises from resistance. The more we try, the heavier we become, the heavier we are the chances of falling down increase.

Just like Nanak - "*Hukum*", like Jesus - "Thy will shall be done" and like Meera - "*Mere to Girdhar Gopal dusro na koi* ", this is acceptance this is complete surrender.

The Ability

Most of the time goes in analysing what and how much has been given to us, comparing with other people, and then arriving to the conclusion that we deserve better or more than what we have.

This is a difference of our ability. We always receive what is best for us, however, it depends on our ability of acceptance that defines the worth of what we receive.

It is the ability that determines our dedication and acceptance as well and then the authority or power rests on it.

Meera's love is an example of her ability. Such immense was her ability that she could amalgamate herself in Mohan, or maybe we can say that Mohan had to become 'Meera'.

Meera opened her eyes and saw a glimpse of Mohan and with her eyes closed she found Mohan within her. It was her ability that she could see Mohan every moment and everywhere.

This was the zenith of her capability to love that despite Mohan's absence, Meera made him a reality.

It is said that Meera did not consider anyone else to be a man other than Mohan. According to her anyone who was in love with Mohan had to be a woman, a feminine energy irrespective of their gender.

Metaphorically we are talking of consciousness. All consciousness is a combination of feminine and masculine energies. There can be women with masculine energy empowering them.

These women will be more of dhyan and karma, determination, or renunciation instead of love and devotion. Similarly, men may have a heart full of love and devotion. They will be more compassionate, will be inclined towards love and devotion and will drop struggles. A heart full of compassion does not require renunciation in the first place. So, here we are talking of our inner abilities.

There is a famous incident related to Meera. When she leaves her palace and starts wandering city to city, from temple to temple and she was about to reach Krishna Temple in Vrindavan.

On knowing of Meera's arrival, the priest gets very angry. The temple did not allow women to enter. The priest tried his best to stop her, but how would anyone stop Meera to enter her Mohan's place, the guards could not work. Priest gets more annoyed of his failure and asks how could she enter the temple when women were not allowed in?

Meera replies, "What devotion is this, when he, the priest could not be friends with Krishna, not a lover not a sakhi?"

Although, the priest got angry, but he understood Meera was talking about the inner capacity which was the only way for a devotee to be one with his Lord.

Lover to the beloved.

The first step towards attaining Krishna and then through him to attain our own self. Actually, Krishna Bhakti is all about love and love is about feminine heart.

Meera knew that Mohan was no other than her own consciousness and this was due to her ability to surrender. The ability that deepened her love and devoutness to wait for Krishna in complete renunciation of all riches and comfort.

Muhammad Sahib sat in the cave of Mount Hira, contemplating for some time, and the first verse descended on him. He felt as if he saw an aura which shone so bright that he could not even see it properly. He saw an impression and just could hear the voice.

At first, he was scared, but the experience was so beautiful, and message so important that he was thrilled to hear. Now he started to wait for the arrival of the messenger, for the messages to arrive. Muhammad Sahib used to sit, meditate in remembrance of the moment when he first experienced it, but now he could not even see a glimpse of it.

It became very difficult for Hazrat Muhammad. He starts to doubt himself, he thought maybe what he had seen earlier was just an illusion. As the days went by, he began to think that he might have gone crazy. The insanity was at an extent when he wanted to wash off the memory also of the incident. He used to share his concern and anxiety with his wife Khadija and she kept on reassuring him that it was not an illusion. She trusted him.

Two years passed and he felt ridiculed as now he was stuck in the storm. Now there was no going back, neither moving ahead.

At times, he also felt that it should not have happened. It was good when he was feeding the camels, taking care of sheep, and living a simple life. But now it was difficult to even survive and he could not understand what to do next.

Three years passed by. In the midst, Hazrat Muhammad started staying ill, his health deteriorated and his serenity began to break. It was again a check on his ability and for now it was his capacity to wait. Initially he had determination and patience, perhaps after a time he started losing them. He kind of believed that the revelation, the Angel and the aura, was just hallucination or a dream.

But again, the miracle happened, again Hazrat Muhammad saw the same aura. Then he heard the same voice that he was waiting for. And then he realised that now is the right time for him to be called the Prophet, the Messenger of Allah.

The revelations he heard from the Holy Angel were supposed to be shared among the people as message from God.

It was this ability of waiting and trust that made Meera a mystical wanderer and Hazrat Muhammad, A Prophet.

Meera proved her ability by announcing Krishna, the non-existent as her beloved. It was also necessary to accept responsibility with this ability and equally important was patience.

Meera chose patience in waiting, love and devotion. In fact, in humiliations or social obligations; she accepted them all with pleasure.

It is said that Meera did not like Radha, she did not like listening about the love affair of Radha and Krishna. But the point is, who would have been Radha for Meera? Meera refused to have the two as existent. The Krishna she knew was all- the divine oneness.

And this ability authorises Meera with the right to call Krishna her husband, her ownership on him and her belongingness to him.

Meera never asked for authority over Krishna as her ability of acceptance and surrender was such that Mohan had to be there for Meera.

Meera's perseverance was not for authority, it was by the ability to surrender that she immersed in Mohan.

Maybe the drape is still tied with the idol of Mohan in the Temple of Dwarika.

Forgiveness

One of the many things very important to learn from the life of Hazrat Muhammad is forgiveness. The harder it is to apologise, the more difficult is to forgive.

Well, here we shall talk about forgiveness and its real worth, however, before that let us have a look at one incident.

Hazrat Muhammad started a mission to unite people, who were divided in smaller groups, under one emblem to strengthen the community and omit rampant violence. Certainly, the power masters were to lose their power and hence, they opposed the movement. He had people walking together with him and at the same time masses who were trouble makers.

The biggest opponents among them were the people of Quraysh Community. These people were so powerful that they did not think it was necessary to be united with anyone and at the same time Mecca, the Holy Shrine also came under their jurisdiction. They feared losing their hold over the shrine if they united with the rest of the tribes.

Every morning when Muhammad Sahib passed through the Quraysh's area, an old woman would throw on him the garbage she collected in her house.

How much she must have hated Muhammad that she collected

the garbage and stored it, waiting for the time when he would pass around her house just to dump the stinking garbage on him. She expressed her anger by doing this.

Then one day it suddenly happened that Hazrat Muhammad passed from there, but the garbage was not thrown on him which caught his attention. The same thing happened again the next day. No one expressed any resentment over him. So, Muhammad Sahib asked the people around about the old lady and he found that the woman was ill.

Muhammad Sahib went inside her house, saw the woman lying ill and helpless. He gave her water to drink and arranged some food for her. He took care of her with full compassion and love as he would do for himself.

The sick lady slowly recovered. Realising Muhammad Sahib's compassion towards her, she felt ashamed of her conduct. With tears in her eyes she went to seek apology from Hazrat Muhammad, smiling 'The Sahib' pardoned her.

It was an apology that we accept from others and share the burden of their guilt and set them free.

But is it not true that in this forgiveness, we are liberating ourselves also somewhere?

It is very important to free ourselves too. Suffering the pain of guilt for our mistakes, we carry life as a burden. It is necessary that we free ourselves from the burden of past events. There are two ways of living, either we can live in misery analysing our mistakes or we can simplify life by learning a lesson from our mistakes in past and moving ahead, collecting the experiences for further reference. Every incident that happens in life does not deserve attention as much as we give. Generally, self-analysis is a positive action however, it leads to our own assassination.

By the way, what is a mistake, what does it mean?

There are efforts, there are actions taken, sometimes there is faith and sometimes there is mistrust. The efforts gone wrong are considered to be mistakes. The truth that remains is at some time or the other, we all make wrong efforts.

Meera forgave all who tried to malign her.

Just like Hazrat Muhammad set the highest recognition of clemency.

Important is that they both along with others forgave themselves too.

Forgiveness, to others as well as to myself.

Just as Muhammad Sahib pardoned the old woman and do not know how many people he accepted despite of their faults; he also forgave himself. Otherwise, he might have failed to perform his duties. How would have he convinced himself to lift a sword? And if he would have failed, Islam was never to be established, people never could have united. They would keep fighting among themselves and dying.

Meera firstly forgave herself. Only then could she dissident. She knew definitely that she was unknowingly hurting her people. But what could she do? Her actions were predetermined.

Once Meera was gifted a basket with a snake inside. She accepted it and forgave her in-laws, her family, for the dreadful act.

In remembrance of her Mohan, holding that basket, she sang her heart out. Shedding tears of joy and devotion, she might have freed her father-in-law from the burden of the inappropriate action. When she opened the basket, she found it full of flowers.

Meera forgave her husband for forsaking her and the society for stigmatising her, and herself too because it was Meera who brought all of it on herself.

Now forgiving and accepting self was most important as all the strength she gathered was from within herself. Her Mohan resided inside her, she never would have wanted to trouble him by living in self-pity and anger. Meera had immense courage and she drove that from the love she had within her.

For this forgiveness, we must first have the capacity to accept our self.

Did Meera ever think of forgiving Mohan? Did Meera ever had a thought that Mohan could never be by her side when she was suffering in his remembrance? Meera was stated wrong always but she had no doubts on her actions. By forgiving and accepting herself, she liberated herself of all the doubts.

She was misunderstood, assassinated based on her character, considered mad and outlawed, but she could understand and forgive all of it because she was the one who was Meera, not everyone else was. So how could have others understood her?

This whole drama in the name of that non-existent, now how would she forgive him? He was never there, she created him.

When are we going to forgive ourselves? We live in guilt, apologising to everyone, we fail to assess self-worth and find faults in self.

Will we be ever apologetic to ourselves? In all, ultimately we treat ourselves the worst.

Freedom- Freeing self

The one who learns to bloom despite being stuck in a marsh is the one who enjoys complete freedom.

The word independence is beautiful and everyone wants to have it, however, it does not come free. Freedom comes with accountabilities. It has positive aspects as well as negative. Freedom also comes with the responsibility for those who live consciously, or maybe freedom itself is a responsibility.

Difference in our situations cause change in our sense of freedom. For someone breaking boundaries can be freedom, for others living within the boundaries can be a sense of belongingness which gives them more confidence.

Years ago, a woman allowed to go out of home to study or work only was the ultimate freedom. In a few Indian states, the veil is so important that freedom for a woman would be when she has the right to keep her head and face uncovered. For a child who enjoys playing a lot, for him being told to study would be a violation of his freedom.

Sometimes we need to be liberated from a person or from some situation, and sometimes thoughts. The truth is that we can want or ask for freedom only from what we see and know.

Will fish living in water ever think about the freedom to fly in the sky? Probably yes, if it comes to know that there is a world outside water, then it definitely would want to see it.

But will that fish out of water survive its independence?

Water and fish are not about relation with subordination or dependency. Water is its life and source of livelihood too. And even if it comes out of the water, will she be able to reach the heights of the sky? And secondly, will this vast sky ever open its arms to that crazy seeker, the fish and allow it some place in its grandeur? No, the laws of nature do not change.

So now it is important to understand that freedom can be found even while living in water. Freedom is not what we believe. Nobody needs to be free from anyone outside. We need to be free from ourselves. Somewhere there is a bond of faith, somewhere of relations, somewhere of religion, somewhere we are engaged in the pursuit of liberation, whereas they never bind us, instead we keep ourselves bound in it.

Freedom is choice or vision, but liberation is not even here for us.

Let's talk of an artist whose art is his passion. He always strived for freedom to continue his passion, which is again sometimes a challenge in society. We expect academic excellence as primary art.

Let's now consider this artist gets the freedom and he is now completely devoted to his art. It is his inspiration, his joy so he fights all odds to pursue and excel the art. Depending upon his enthusiasm towards his art he gradually starts earning fame. This art is also his freedom of expression and the same skill gives him confidence to decide his way.

However, he may not realise that he is being trapped even in the fame that he earns from freedom. Later his identity gets associated with the fame -a complete bondage.

The one who seeks freedom from past or for future, freedom from fear or stress, may never really be free. Liberated from one, they may fall in another trap. Utmost requirement of freedom is freedom from the self.

The same liberation as Meera did.

Meera! What comes to mind as soon as you read this name? Mohan's Meera? Krishna's devotee?

Strangely, despite Mohan's absence Meera is still called as Mohan's Meera.

Wow! How mistaken we are, it was not about Mohan's Meera. She was always Meera's Meera because the two never happened. Meera was alone and Mohan was the foundation of Meera's path of aloneness that she chose for herself. The path on which Meera discovered herself.

We could not understand the freedom that gave Meera the power to surrender in depths and the heights of devotion. And then Meera took up her own responsibility leaving behind all the burdens of judgement.

Meera enjoyed wandering with sages and dancing and singing for her Mohan. These were forbidden acts for a Queen of the Royal family. She was never forsaken for this liberation that she allowed herself, but of course she had decided, so who would stop? She had tasted bliss in this, she learned to live through it.

She was neither flattered by appreciation nor bothered of maliciousness. And for this freedom, she did not seek any support from anyone other than her *chitta shakti* known as Mohan.

Meera considered Sant Ravidasji to be her Guru or mentor. She used to listen to Krishna's stories, *Krishna-leela*, from him. Both sat for hours together. Ravidasji narrated many stories about Krishna and that's how Meera used to meet her Mohan.

Ravidasji belonged to lower caste, a shoemaker. For a Queen to hobnob with a lower caste man was an act of rebellion.

But how could Meera stop? It was about Mohan, and in his celebration, nothing could stop her.

Once Ravidasji was narrating a story about Krishna soaked in devotion and Meera quenching her thirst and exploring her own depths while listening to him.

At that time Ravidasji was also polishing a piece of leather completely rejoicing his Krishna with Meera as a disciple. His hand slipped in such a way that some droplets of water used for polishing the leather splashed on Meera's sari, her drape.

Ravidasji said, *Hey Meera, tu to saanwre ka rang me rang gyi... Meera,* Krishna has accepted you as his own!

And abnormally mad Meera picked her Ektara and started singing, *Main Sanvare ke rang rachi....*

Meera was beyond variances of caste, religion and name. These made no difference to her as ultimately it was her own depths that she was exploring and her own heights she was wavering in.

Call her of Mohan or Hazrat Muhammad's, truth is she was free, even in the deep sea and the vast sky.

Do we remember that rock? Who was liberated as Ahilya on the touch of Rama? Was Ahilya independent? Or the rock that was waiting for Rama to touch it was freer?

Some such freedom is seen in routine life that only looks like freedom but

It is not.

At least that rock must have had the freedom to wait. **This waiting was wilful, so it was freedom?** ***Could this waiting still be considered as freedom if Rama would have never arrived?***

The Mysterious Nomads

A common connection between Meera and Muhammad. What was it? Spirituality, devotion? These come later.

If anyone is asked about common connection between Meera and Muhammad, perhaps, their first thought would be a difference, difference of religion. However, for now we are not discussing the differences. We are talking of similarities, and there are many.

Moving towards similarity, first thought will be of spirituality, which certainly is right.

Out of many, one common connection, never spoken about is the 'Desert'.

They both belonged to the land of sand. Both were travellers and wanderers who were lost in the desert. Both shared similar melody in life. The melody underlying in the desert. The hidden secrets that influenced their lives. The belief they both shared, the non-existent 'HIM' and the reason of this shared belief was the desert that was infinite.

This desert is the witness of their journey of love, compassion, devotion and more. What makes the desert even more mysterious are the stories that are buried within it that can be heard in the dense and serene nights.

In the desert, we see the engraved secrets of warriors who fought battles with bravery, yet in the end they surrendered themselves into the lap of their mother land. Many hearts that beat for other but could not rest on each-other's shoulders hence, found their solace in being lost in the desert. Hidden beneath are the screams of lovers and beloved.

The desert has hidden many secrets under the layers of sand. Whenever a storm hits the desert, the layer grows even thicker; deepening the mystery.

The desert has its own rhythm, its own notes which is acknowledged as one of the best folk music.

The music that establishes connection between one world and another. It has its own dance. The whirling, practiced by Sufi dervish comes from desert. The way the whirlpool of the storm soars high and travels fast, similarly you transit from one edge to another, from mind to the mindlessness while whirling. That moment of ultimate paradise would have always been hidden in the wilderness of desert.

However, this gift of whirling that was popularised by Sufi mystics, has brought one more way to bliss for spirituality seekers. Similarly, Meera's dance, too, is one example of this ecstasy.

The mystery that is spread across acres of sand; meeting the edges with the horizon, to the end of sight, what is visible is 'golden sand', rest all is hidden.

The sand shines brightly when sunlight falls on it, like a kiss of affection on the forehead of a beloved planted by her lover, both soaked in devotion for each other. The moment sun sets in the dusk, the entire desert turns into a calm and peaceful land as if a smile on the face of a baby in deep sleep. May be the smile on the child's face is due to the remembrance of the journey that's been there for innumerable lives.

For the innocent child is aware that it is the same soul that travels from one to another body. The soul is one, it remains same.

Heat and aridity of this piece of land has lots of unsaid stories lying under it and colder nights hold tight the chilling and jaw dropping mysteries under the thick sheet of the moving sand.

Yes, moving sand as no one as of now could ever hold a fist full of sand. The more firmly and tightly we try to hold it, the faster it slips. Although the land is divided and marked, however, no one standing at one end has yet seen the other end of a desert.

Born in Marwar of Rajasthan, Meera could understand the melody of this desert. Wandering gave her more pleasure than staying still. She knew that the palace is just a worldly affair. A woman of wisdom, she found bliss in exploring herself, roaming in the desert that hummed the secrets of life.

Muhammad Sahib, years ago, explored the desert in a similar manner. Performing his duties, fulfilling responsibilities and yet exploring his true self, finding the One supreme, shapeless and formless.

Desert was the sole observer of their journeys, of the cosmic oneness they experienced. Numerous battles fought by

Muhammad Sahib, his compassion towards human, the law of sharing practiced by him and then the sacrifice of his grandsons and loved ones, to all of these, the desert was a witness. His sermons that were the revelations he had in his life time and then sharing his words of wisdom; the desert stored these memories.

Meera, who arrived after years, again she was a believer of that formless energy. That omnipresent HIM who she said was her husband. Her songs and poetries in the longingness of her beloved Mohan, are all safely treasured in the desert. These deserts were the sole companion in her dance and devotion for the name she gave to her own formless divine.

She the lover, she the beloved.

Maybe once again this will sound disturbing, here this cosmic oneness is not about amalgamation, it is about the oneness of journey, beliefs and devotion. Acceptance of the non-existent soul. Only the one who is compassionate towards all the creations would be able to see the beauty of the desert, else for us the beauty remains in rivers and mountains. Oceans and Himalayas will be the representation of love. The ones who have seen the depths and heights both together, will be only able to see the beauty in the aridity of the desert. The ones who rise in love instead of falling in it, will see themselves one with the infinite.

The way Meera reached the heights of devotion wandering in the desert is an example of the compassion she beheld in her heart; and so did Muhammad Sahib. Both together set an extraordinary spirit of remembrance and reverence.

This reverence works as hope; a ray of hope for a traveller stuck in the desert and he suddenly sees greenery somewhere afar. His heart fills with gratitude towards the unknown who has shown a miracle; a source of life in the desert. Same green could have been the colour of Meera's veil while she was drowned in her love for Mohan; and the same green that years back was colour of Muhammad Sahib's emblem.

One soul for the whole

That omnipresent who resides within us, he is the one we spend our whole life searching for, although he stays within us only. That one who is for all....

One soul for the whole.

Now see, there is no difference between Ram and Raheem because the one inside them is same.

These differences are all just opinions inculcated in us over a period of time due to manmade differences.

We all are humans and our basic trait is love and compassion for one another, to celebrate the life to the fullest.

There is a small incident from Muhammad Sahib's life where Muhammad and Mohan come across at the same time, not Mohan as an appearance, but as an invisible source, as an energy, as a consciousness.

As of now, we are aware Muhammad Sahib had to fight innumerable battles to establish the Muslim polity. These fights were not a result of his hunger for power. Those days, people were divided under various kabila (groups) who had their own leaders. These kabilas used to fight with each other to steal the wealth for their own livelihood. There were trade wars between them, abduction of women and massive killings by the stronger kabilas. Weaker ones feared the stronger ones as strong one tortured the weaker one and looted the little wealth they had.

All these kabilas not only had different leaders, they also had different Gods in form of idols. Those days the situation was such that people used to travel for trade and barter and the Holy Mecca was a centre for caravans traveling. All the caravans carried with them an idol of the god they worshipped and found it auspicious to place that idol at the Holy Mecca. Quraysh, one of the most powerful kabilas, were the custodians of this sacred shrine.

While growing up, Muhammad Sahib was a witness to all the rampant violence and loot. Therefore, he intended to bring all the small and powerful kabilas under one polity which was Islam. Hence the religion was established as one, believers of one God.

In process, first of all he had to abolish this idol worship, different Gods for different tribes.

The union witnesses bloodshed.

Hence, he started preaching the formless god saying 'Allah is invisible'. There is no deity as an idol. The biggest challenge for Muhammad Sahib was to unite with Quraysh and it was equally important as Mecca was the centre for trade. It took him several attempts of battle to win over the Quraysh. They were strong, rich and larger community. After eight years of constant trials, he could enter Mecca, although later he returned to Medina, leaving his birth place.

Now the incident says, Quraysh had declared a bounty (reward) on the killing of Muhammad Sahib.

The battle again happened between Quraysh and Mohammad Sahib's people. Motivated for the prize, this was the most violent battle as all were prepared to kill Muhammad Sahib.

All those with Muhammad Sahib were already dead in fight, only his friend Abu Bakar was left alive. To save their lives Muhammad Sahib and Abu Bakar hid in a cave. We need to stop and reflect here, why Muhammad Sahib chose to hide and save his life instead of letting go of it? The reason is that he was aware that his responsibilities were pending.

People were still finding them. It is said that the moment they entered a spider cobwebbed the entrance and the ones who were behind them to kill felt that no one could enter that cave as there was no passage.

Yet they were so violent, blinded in greed, they tried their hands on the spider web and later left assuming that if anyone was inside would be dead or at least injured to die.

During this incident Abu Bakar tells Muhammad Sahib, that only two of them could survive.

On that Muhammad Sahib says, 'we are three'. Surprised Abu Bakar replied "we are only two here, we have lost all our men".

Then Muhammad Sahib says, 'the one who wanted us to be safe, he who brought us here, is also with us, the third invisible one.'

Do we know who this 'the one' was?

The Mohan of Meera, the formless non-existent. This incident nullifies the gaps of time and birth. This incident is an example of oneness of souls and its presence.

The Mohan, the Krishna of Mahabharat, the one whose Bhagvad Gita is a prophecy for the living. In a dialogue between Sri Krishna and Arjun in the battle field, Lord Krishna stated that:

"Dharma Sansthapanarthaya Sambhavami Yuge yuge"

Whenever troublemakers are busy destroying the world order or to harm Dharma, the Lord incarnates with the purpose to put everything in proper balance. To restore order. His compassion is the main reason for Lord's incarnation. As per Gitopdesh the Lord said he will appear again and again on this planet as a chit-shakti- Consciousness in every living and non-living being. It's the consciousness that travels from one to another, then where is the difference in Meera's Mohan and Muhammad and even Meera herself?

It was the same consciousness that once appeared as Krishna, then as Muhammad and Meera too. Today the same Chaitanya is in all of us. We just fail to recognise it, and in a way, to recognise ourselves.

Now this consciousness that we all share is beyond the worldly bonds and obligations. The Chaitanya is not bound in relationships and expectations. It is the same in all. The father and the daughter share same consciousness.

The bond that Meera shared with her Mohan, the lord and the devotee; the lover and the beloved was between the same souls and the same consciousness that was within Muhammad Sahib too.

Meera always believed in Muhammad Sahib's preaching, the Lord was always invisible for Meera. Formless, non-existent. So, did not Meera mean exactly what Muhammad Sahib established centuries and years before Meera's existence?

Did not Mohan mean the same when he said he would reincarnate as Chaitanya to control the devastations. Mohan in his conversation at the battle field of Mahabharata, says that we must fight for the good of mankind even though it is with our own people. Purpose is most important and if the reason is right, no deed can be wrong.

Now, here we need a little correction. Once again, we may go to the religious difference as Gita is said to be a Hindu Holy Scripture, however, where does lord Krishna say that he is only for Hinduism and, where is any mention of religious differences? Bhagvad Gita is a prophecy for life, and the creator is one.

He who created all of us is one, then why are we trying to find the presence or existence in a particular religion? Mohan and Muhammad may walk together, may walk with- in each other.

Is not the soul one?

Un-Identifying the Identity

Who is Meera without her Mohan?

Is that a question in our minds?

It happens, when your love and devotion grow deeper, the other becomes more significant, so much that you start considering them The God, The Supreme. Exactly that was what was happening with Meera. Why Meera still cannot be assumed without Krishna, has no other reason than this.

Meera has been identified with Mohan so much that it is impossible for us to accept her without Him. Although if we understand it in another way, Krishna for Meera was a consciousness, her own Chaitanya, probably what she named as Krishna.

As we are aware Krishna never existed with Meera. Krishna was a state of pure devotion that liberated Meera. The state of love, which is why it is said that Meera considered Krishna as her husband which was nothing but her own state of being.

If we try to understand consciousness, actually there cannot be an external source of any form that can persuade a human to the heights of devotion and madness that was seen in

Meera. It is always our own hidden consciousness or sub consciousness that derives us to reach the divinity.

No one saw Mohan in Meera's presence. What they always saw was Meera's devotion behind the closed doors of the temple, or in her singing or in the melody of her anklets while wandering in desert.

The same infinite desert was inside Meera in form of pure mindfulness. Meera never was even interested to prove the presence of Kanha, for she knew that it was her individual journey which driven by the source that she named as Kanha, her own inner strength.

Now for Meera, Mohan's physical presence was insignificant. It did not matter whether Krishna was there or not, whether he was her object of love or devotion. Meera was complete within herself.

In fact, probably Meera is the one who makes Krishna, it is always a devotee who makes lord, a lover who makes the beloved more significant than them. Ultimately, this is the only way to achieve higher consciousness. When the other is more important, the ego disappears and gradually we too and the lord too. In that vanishing, we find the true meaning of presence. Although, it is very difficult to happen. Why because, when love happens, the 'I' still exists, in devotion too, the devotee exists. This vanishing is the real transformation, once we disappear, we realise and discover the soul that is one in all. It's not I, not HIM, its one in all.

Now as we know that in the journey, ultimate realisation is when we discover the self. For this discovery, the transformation that we spoke about is a process.

Meera lived for Krishna, who was not there ever in physical form, but in this devotion, she freed herself.

In her freedom from the self, she found the strength to nullify the social structure, although even in modern day society, we are carrying the social obligation. She became a model of empowerment. Empowerment not in terms of position or strength. Empowerment in terms of depth. In terms of belief and in terms of consciousness.

Her family, the society, all kept on disapproving of Meera's actions, yet she had the power to choose and to proceed on what she found was right. Forsaking the luxuries and deciding to wander around made her rebellious and she still is a flag-bearer of female liberation.

What was that source which gave her the strength to challenge the society more than five hundred years ago?

All she had was the power of complete surrender and devotion.

The madness worked as her strength to unfold the one who was always present within her.

Again, here we see a common quality in Mohan, Muhammad and Meera. They all choose their own path, walked on them dropping the fear of judgement.

Krishna, on the one hand disappeared and overnight established the kingdom in Dwarika to escape war with Jarasandh after multiple defeats as Jarasandh had decided to kill Krishna and Balaram and finish the Yadav vansh (dynasty). After seventeen such attempts by Jarasandh, lord decided to hide away. He never feared to be called coward for this act, the *Ranchhor*

On the other hand, Muhammad Sahib fought numerous battles which were required to strengthen the community but this was also known as an act of cruelty. He never feared the judgements again. Meera, was an example of a ferocious rebel to walk against social norms.

They have similarities, they have differences, however they are all complete in their own way. Then why does Meera need Mohan to establish her? Actually, she does not.

The journey of madness to abnormal madness, Meera spent dancing.

Sanity or abnormal madness

Madness needs to occur in totality. Incomplete madness leads us nowhere.

That's what we learn from Meera. A seer's devotion is also a form of madness. A madness that takes one to the state of complete no mind.

Sanity is wise, it knows the direction. Whereas, the directionless flow is what contemplation is. This directionless flow ultimately reaches to the destination.

Drowned in love, floating in devotion, if we can still think, if we can still realise, we are sane. If we still can feel that we are mad, we are living in sanity. This means that we have begun the journey, however, the moment this sanity dilutes, the discovering starts. The reality starts unfolding. The merging begins.

Meera's saree wrapped around the idol of Krishna in the temple of Dwarika cannot be a result of sanity.

Then, what was Meera, who was she? She was an abnormal mad, an insane wanderer.

This abnormality is precious.

Madness is a state where you can still control your thoughts as you are aware of them, being called a mad matters to you. Abnormal madness makes you completely free. Total liberation happens when you naturally start giving up, in fact you do not even give up, and you simply lose or begin living up. When you start accepting the way things arrive to you effortlessly. The flow, the direction without any resistance and maybe you are even unaware of this acceptance.

That is what the course of Meera's life suggests. She could not fake to be in sync with society. She did not plan her actions in order to lead a comfortable life.

She accepted herself and led the way as her devotion for Mohan directed sequence of her life.

She wavered and lost the control completely in saintliness and let herself pour in the vessel of divinity. The way her inner consciousness directed, she was persuaded towards devoutness, smoothly.

A beautiful incident of her life, where in Meera was offered a bowl of poison, she consumes the whole poison, without asking a single question. This incident was an example of her heights of surrender and devotion towards her lord, which was the result of her insanity. Had she have had a state of sanity, she would have given a thought before doing so. However, she had complete faith in Mohan, the one who was always within her. Maybe she could have died that day, still, she would never have a doubt as maybe she knew, whatever would happen, will still be in accord with the divine.

May be in her state of no mind, there was no difference between poison and nectar. Maybe her insanity was aware that everything is pre-decided.

In her divinity, she was already in terms with herself to understand the mystery of life.

Some would see it as courage, some as spiritual powers, however, clearly, it is a complete abnormal madness. Devotion certainly leads to higher levels of madness, which is abnormal one.

Spiritual awakening is invalid context when it comes to Meera. For her only state was no mind, the abnormal madness. Love itself is a crazy thing. With Meera, we see lots of threads attached to love, and most important was realisation of self.

Even in devotion, we may still recover, however, Meera had no way of coming back from her insanity. Probably she was even beyond a devout or a lover.

Meera's insanity made her highly unique. Her abnormal love and devotion make her stand apart even today when we talk about devotees.

A story says, that Mohan himself arrived to guide Meera to visit Vrindavan and stay there for some time. It was once when Meera felt broke, her faith might have shaken as there was certainly a lot to deal with. For once she might have thought of ending her life. And the one she was taking it all for was never there to help her collect the broken pieces of her soul.

But it was just that one moment and Mohan appeared to show her some light. Maybe that was her own inner voice that appeared as ***Chitt Shakti***, the power of inner consciousness. The Mohan in Meera.

Meera, A Celebrated Disgrace

Talking of consciousness, Meera was no less than many that we have read or heard of. An enlightened mystic was Meera.

Although, she is one of the most celebrated saints, a pioneer of liberation for women, still is she accepted in society? Why does she still need a name of someone to represent her, although her entire life is a model of self-search? Is it just her gender?

Maybe Krishna, if mythologies are to be believed, he himself never might have discriminated among genders. The Hindu religion worships goddess as source of energy, Shakti. Shiva can be seen in ***ardhnariswar avatar***. Then too how come the discrimination so strongly prevails in the culture?

Let's talk about the time of Adam and Eve, when no traces of manhood were there on the earth, these two of different genders were sent to the Garden of Eden. The Biblical story says that Adam and Eve were free to eat fruits from the whole garden except of one tree. Eve meets a talking serpent who deceives her to eat the fruit of the forbidden tree. Poor Eve was unaware of the intentions of this serpent, it was a shaitan. Eve gives the fruit to Adam also which arouses sexual desire in them.

Although, Man and Woman in the Garden of Eden were sent by the creator with a purpose to begin life and start the worldly affair. All by themselves, these two, unknown about their nakedness, roaming around together in the garden might have had curiosity about each other. Those moments of loneliness and a general feeling of curiosity might have led them to physical intimacy. However, that was a sinful act as per God. Hence they had to be punished. Here again was a discrimination of gender, the women were cursed with pain at the time of childbirth and man to overpower her at the times of sexual act. For the same act, if women were to be punished, how could man be rewarded with more power? Was it because of that fruit which Eve offered to Adam or for being innocent to trust the shaitan?

Although, reproduction was the requirement of the time and was much needed for the beginning of world, then too man and woman were punished differently for same sin. In fact man was set free. Is this not strange?

In all this process, a man and a woman were supposed to be together. To start life together, to explore bliss together, and to achieve consciousness together. Sexuality is the source of transcendence. From reproduction to spirituality, everywhere a man and a woman need to be in accordance, but where did we start the discrimination from?

Anyways before we proceed further, here we need to understand that touch and feel are strongest emotions. Most appropriate way of expression.

Sex, although not accepted by society, but it is a divine act. It is one act that opens the doors to super consciousness, if accepted fully. The ecstatic state that we reach to, if ever we do, is the time of surrender in totality.

But as it is observed that when we fail to reach to that state of bliss through this expression, during sexual act, it brings frustration, sadness, and anguish.

This situation could be the one that introduced mankind to other sources of pleasure, delight, and trance. If the man failed the orgasmic bliss, they found the other ways of seeing no mind, which were introduced as various forms of meditation, whirling, and artistry. Hence even for spiritual awakening, both play similarly an important role.

Why Muhammad can have a religion and Meera should be forgotten despite one of the most fabulous journeys? Why cannot Muhammad and Meera walk together?

When the same soul exists in Meera and Muhammad, why cannot Meera be accepted for her courage and devoutness the way Muhammad Sahib is.

Why Muhammad Sahib a prophet for community and Meera a disgrace for family?

Muhammad Sahib is remembered for the sacrifices he made, is Meera too for her devotion?

Ultimately, when the soul is one, when Meera and Muhammad are in each one of us, why can't she be respected and accepted in the same way?

Meera has already established an example of women's empowerment. Power not in terms physical strength; power in terms of devotion. Strength to rebel, courage to sacrifice. All the women's empowerment activities happening today stand futile as Meera had already empowered women centuries ago.

Man and Woman have always been the complementary sources of energy.

Does Meera need an introduction supported by anyone else? Krishna never existed for Meera, she was always complete, as a courageous wanderer.

Art of Surrender-Quran begins from here

Meera's journey is an example of total surrender. Her transformation to the saintliness was a result of her complete devotion to Mohan. She mastered this art of surrender, as it was the only way of discovering herself. Her surrender was completely unique as Krishna was not present in reality, in a physical form, still her devotion was such that she entirely submerged in her love for Krishna, and liberated herself completely.

Thus, Meera became an enlightened source of Bhakti. In fact, Meera herself became synonymous with devotion.

When you give up your will completely to God's willingness that is the art of surrender. To be more specific, it is wilful acceptance of what happens with complete faith in a fact that whatever happens has a bigger purpose than what we understand.

So, does Muhammad Sahib say, "the art of surrender is the only way of attainment", and he suggest all to follow the same.

Prayer in Islam is nothing, but a form of surrender, 'submission to god', again to the invisible omnipresent, formless.

Meera never questioned the events that took place in her life. She never doubted her life, her journey. She lived in total acceptance and belief that whatever she came across was the only way to reach to the one residing deep within her, whom she called Girdhar Gopal.

This complete trust, that lets one flow in the direction of wind without even trying to hold the branches is what surrender is.

Meera kept on flowing in the love; sometimes caught in a whirlpool; sometimes drowning in Yamuna River, but she knew the merging takes place when the identity dissolves. So much that first, the person dissolves into a disciple, then from a disciple to devotee, later from a devotee to devout and then even the devout dissolves and they become one identity, one soul. Then the ultimate Chaitanya is discovered.

The lover and beloved dissolve in each other and become total Love and devotion.

Her devotion and surrender to her Krishna were complete and this clearly reflects in Meera's beautiful poems. In Meera's poetry we often come across her requesting about the complete solvency when Krishna accepts her as a celebrated servant, to serve him.

She says, "*Shyam mane chakar rakho ji...*Shyam, accept me as your servant, having done that, you grant me a chance for having your glimpse, anytime, anywhere, every time and everywhere, even in the middle of night. You give me a chance to sing your leela to the world and allow everyone a chance to witness the ecstasy of transcendence".

While talking of this extreme devotion and this surrender, Meera talks about the Miracle that is happening within her in the presence of this total consciousness. As the consciousness is a matter of within, hence this surrender also comes right from there, and stays there. This source of strength triggers thousands suns in her vast inner sky and in that light she sees herself, as a reflection of Krishna -- the Chaitanya.

It is said that, when Meera left the palace and went to Vrindavana and Mathura. She spent most of her time praying and worshipping Lord Krishna. She kept wandering in search of enlightenment. Finally, she went to Dwarika.

Her love for Krishna was so deep that, it is said that, she disappeared in the temple of Krishna in Dwarika, merged in idol of his beloved.

She always carried her Krishna within her. She might have never searched for him outwards, she had already surrendered to him, hence there was no way to search for him, and she was searching herself. Yes, she left the palace, maybe because she knew that her home was somewhere else. The pleasure was in flowing instead of stopping at one place.

Meera had no insecurities; when the most treasured one was within her, what was there to lose? The most important self, she had surrendered to the self. Now wherever this invisible self was taking, the visible one was just following, in complete acceptance. In complete surrender. This surrender gives us the privilege to enjoy our privileges, privilege of authority, to the fullest. A right to insist, to express and to say that:

You are mine and I am yours,

My heart is a home for you,

And in your eyes, I see myself,

I for you and you for me and that is the complete world around us.

The rights that we gain moving from love to surrender, that really is not the question of rights in real sense, but it is more about acceptance. However, it is much sequential and conditional. The acceptance and submission if happen, then only we can talk of rights or authority. It is earned not asked for, cannot be stolen or snatched.

Meera loved the idol form of Krishna and she attained herself through that form. She had no need or expectations, she did not desire anything from Krishna in exchange of her devotion; she simply goes on giving, and what best a devotee can give than to surrender her own self. She had a song to sing, she sings. She had a dance to offer, she danced but with no expectation, no questions. She has nothing to get, she only gives, and yet she gets a thousand times.

The five pillars of Islam talk about professing Faith, Prayer, Alms giving or charity, Fasting during the holy month of Ramadan or pilgrimage to Mecca, these all pillars are in a way an example of complete surrender to God's will.

Muhammad and Meera both were skilled in the art of surrender; else who can be so selfless to leave the stature and live up to hermitage that Meera did and who would live by the belief that who he wants us to wake up the next day, arranges for the next day, and preaches that there was nothing more satisfying than to see a smile on the face of the needy. Muhammad Sahib never saved for the next day.

This belief in Giver also ultimately is the belief in self.

Meera, A state of Cultural consciousness

Searching the self to dissolving in self

The Rana shouted at Meera, saying, "Meera, show me your lover with whom you were talking now".

Meera replies, "There sits He-my Lord-the *Nayanchora* who has stolen my heart" and she slips into a state of trance, unconscious.

Who was there? Thinks Rana, completely perplexed, and confused.

There was no one. Then whom did he hear Meera speaking with? Not only Rana, others too have heard several times. The one seated there was an idol. And, how could one speak to the idol and then be so much devoted to live in a state of trance.

This was Meera, she was beyond the equations of physical presence. Perhaps, she was aware that till the time the second one is present, you cannot be really 'one' with beloved.

People around used to float rumours of Meera's ill character as Meera was freely socialising with the Sadhus. Accusations from royal family members too did not worry her. When questioned about her marital responsibilities, Meera responded that she was married to Krishna. However, Krishna was not even present for a while. In his absence, who made him present was Meera. Meera made the Mohan, or may be the Mohan emerged in Meera.

This is a strange reality, Meera was a rebel who could decide to leave her family, her marital responsibilities and carry on her spiritual journey with much pride within her consciousness, her innate Krishna.

Yes, Krishna was innate in her, maybe in the form of a characteristic. This could be one reason why it was never important for her to have Krishna by her side. She never tried owning him, possessing him, she just celebrated him beyond the extremes of devoutness.

Maybe due to the societal pressure or responsibilities, she would have had to abandon Krishna, if he was a second person, someone who existed outside her. Meera was beyond individuality, beyond physical presence.

Let us now think of a situation which is often seen. There are few among us who, at some point in time, knew that the life they were living was not worth living, not something that is real. A few out of those some, at some point in time, even thought of leaving it all behind and starting on another journey.

However, most of them, as it often happens, ignored the inner calling and continued with the same journey in life. As we all know that the worldly responsibilities that we have planned or set for ourselves cannot be ignored.

Now, at this point, we need to stop and think. How did Meera leave her worldly obligations to continue with her journey? Because there was no one else who could understand her acceptance of the non-existence and her search of self, whereas at the same time Meera was absolutely sure and aware of her quest. Now the worldly obligations did not stand relevant to her.

Despite all odds, she never abandoned her Krishna because how could one abandon oneself when there was no other? There is a belief that still prevails that a woman needs to be supported, she needs to be held. Why can't she have her own light?

Meera denied the misconceptions long ago.

The turning point in Meera's life happened when once The Great Akbar and his court musician Tansen arrived Chittor, astonished to know of Meera's devotional and inspiring songs as they had heard about Meera and her mysticism. Both entered the temple and listened to Meera's soul - stirring songs to their heart's content. Before Emperor Akbar departed, he touched the holy feet of Meera.

The Rana was furious. He told Meera, "Drown yourself in the river and never show your face to the world in the future. You have brought great disgrace on my family".

"I feel a total connection with him. I cannot break that bond," replies Meera. This him was the one in her.

Although there is no evidence to prove the above episode, however, this has been said and explained many a times.

Maybe Meera's love for Krishna, in Rana's understanding brought disgrace to a caring husband that Rana was. For it was not easy for anyone else other than Meera herself to understand this unrestricted flow of emotions, devoutness and sensuality.

Meera walked barefoot on the burning sand and scorching heat of Rajasthan.

Meera is admired and revered and till date survives in the Cultural Consciousness of the people.

Times have changed, yet the beliefs are the same. We are still unable to accept a woman's vulnerability as her strength and at the same time a person's devotion needs to be given a name.

Whereas Meera always had her own light. She was in the search of self. The journey of her wandering has always explained that we all have a chance to become Meera. Like Budhhahood, Meera is a state of devotion, to complete surrender to the inner consciousness. The Chitta Shakti.

You may name it Mohan, Muhammad or anyone else, we are routing ourselves to Meera.

The Dense Mystique Mist

Dried flowers scattered on the grave,

And the ashes in the crematorium found the address to home,

Spread like a soft carpet at 'HIS' footsteps,

There was a mystery hidden in them

Flowers ask the ashes, why do you whirl around HIM?

Ashes answer, this is what the question is.

Ultimately, we have found the beloved and our sacred home

Love is drowning in the be-loved and the dense mist is now beautiful

Let's fragment in HIS fragrance and celebrate ourselves

Having nectar of HIS presence through his eyes

Meera's scripture is of love, devotion and surrender. Meera's lesson in fact is less a scripture, more of music. Only through music can the scripture of devotion be written. Just as logic becomes the scripture of knowledge, music becomes the scripture of devotion. Just as science is the basis of knowledge, similarly poetry is foundation for dissolution in devotion. The knower seeks the truth, but the devotee searches for love, not truth. In fact, love is the only truth for a seeker, only love is truth for the devotee.

The *gyani* says *Satyam Shivam Sundaram.* The devotee says that love is the truth and it is beautiful too.

And what is the truth of acceptance, of surrender?

If we are ready to burn our heart, and smell the fragrance rising from it, only then would we be able to understand the relation of ashes and flowers on the grave. Tasting the nectar of the presence of the beloved through his eyes despite of his absence, was exactly what Meera did.

Anyway, there is nothing else in the world that is more important than love.

Meera had a life of uncertainty and she was ready to dwell in the infinite love that has no end. Those who can give up themselves in the search of their own are the ones who can survive the uncertainties, however, at the same time their possibilities are infinite. Meera had this power, this determination and she exceled in the art of surrender.

Meera is like a river. Nothing could be more pure and immaculate than her. But it seems that we have lost an opportunity. An opportunity to learn to let drown and lose ourselves in love. This losing too was an accomplishment of self.

Meera is not about relationships or marital bondage. Meera is about marital bliss, a union of love and soul. Beyond the rituals, an affair of quietness. Here we do not need scared fire, no temple, no church, no vermillion and no garlands.

The only knot is of love and devotion tied with dedication in the presence of our own soul as witness. She gave a different meaning to marriage and love. Again, in this she did not need a companion, the promises made to Mohan were really to her own self. In this divine union, the only celebration was of the self and Meera kept singing, *"Jake sar mor mukut... Mero pati soi"*- The one who owns peacock feather in his crown is my husband, she addressed Krishna.

Meera's this association with Mohan was her pride and delight. Where there was no fear of separation neither she had to prove her love at any point. She considered herself complete in the absence of her beloved whom she always found present within her.

May be the love that was right there since forever. Meera has nothing to do with logic and intelligence. Meera can only be understood by seeing with emotion, with devotion, with the eyes of reverence. The love that stays like silver lining in sky does not have any law and rules.

Humming Krishna, sinking with Krishna, floating with him, living in him, Meera is all about insanity, and madness. If we have the courage to dive into the insanity, there could be chances that we may understand her.

Go crazy with Meera for a while in her world of joy. This is a world of lovers once we enter it, then we will find that Meera has no connection with the outside world. These are the vibrations of the devotee; they are only related to the inner world.

Meera is just a serene manifestation of emotion. Emotions that created poetries, and dance. Unpolished, raw diamonds that Meera gave to the world.

It is said that Meera was an incarnation of a Gopi, Lalita. She used to sing with Krishna in Vrindavan, danced with Krishna. This love is old - Meera also says the same - This love cannot be new. And Meera's journey clearly states that such a bond and love is not a matter of a day. It is a submission of ages, incarnations.

Meera was a little girl when her family had a visitor, a sadhu who stayed with them overnight. Next morning, Meera watches him take out an idol from his bag and he starts to worship. Something amazing happens, as if she suddenly remembered something, the idol attracted Meera towards it. She wanted it anyhow.

She feels that in the idol, she sees herself and she insists to the guest that he give her the idol. That idol was of Mohan – and this love story was to flourish again. This also was a beginning of an end for Meera, with this she was reincarnated. She weeps and cries, however, the visitor refuses to give her the idol. Meera's heart aches, but the visitor leaves her home, taking the idol with him. Days go by. Meera could not forget the dark eyed Mohan and his peacock feathered crown. A disheartened Meera falls ill.

The visitor, too, had great affection to the idol, letting it go was difficult for him.

One night, the visitor sadhu has a dream. He sees the same idol of Krishna who tells him to handover the idol to the one it belongs. The idol must go to the one who has heart for the idol. The sadhu was astonished. He had been worshipping the same idol for many years but he never had a glimpse of the lord. Now he appears to him in a dream, that too with a command that he would not wish to obey.

Nonetheless, he goes to Meera's house again and gives her the idol with heavy heart.

Krishna had come alive for Meera and she wanted nothing else. She played with the idol, spoke with it, and shared her joy and disagreements with it. She kept the idol next to her while she slept in the night.

Two years later, someone was getting married in the neighbourhood, and this seven or eight-year-old girl asks her mother who will be my groom?

Her mother looks at Meera who was standing holding Krishna's idol close to her chest. Her mother repeats, "Who will be your groom?? This Girdhar Gopal, he is your groom! What else do you want?"

These words sow the seeds of a revolution.

From that day on, Meera pours all her love at the feet of Krishna. The more the love she poured; the more Mohan became alive. Initially, she used to talk alone, later Krishna too starts to talk with her, as if he responded to her love. At first, she danced alone, then Krishna too grooves with her. This was no more a relationship of devotee and idol; it was of devotee and God -- the Lover and the Beloved.

Meera loved Mohan with all her being. She had intense love for him and lived soaked in emotions for Mohan. Meera was attached to her mother who passed away while she was very young. Then Baba raises her. Later, he too passes away. Now just Mohan was the focus of her love and affection. She could only belong to Mohan. Her world shrank and it was all around Mohan, the divine grew larger.

Along with this, these incidents of deaths of her loved ones taught a very important lesson to Meera. Everything in this world was uncertain, she could realise. So, instead of searching outwardly, why not search for something eternal? Nothing was permanent in the worldly order. Why to entangle here? Even breath was temporary and death is the only truth. Everything else was just an act.

Now Krishna only meant love and devotion for her. Love of a formless form. Acceptance of absence that was permanent.

Initially, Meera danced in the house, with the idol of Krishna. Then love augmented like a storm and the house could not contain it. Then Meera started dancing in the village, in temples, in the groups of saints and *satsangis*, as well as in the desert. Then, love became so intense that she could not be cognizant.

She was merry, she was engrossed, and she was enchanted. It was a euphoric state Meera lived in. She surrendered herself both devotionally and in bodily form to Mohan saying that she belonged only to him.

She was so much absorbed in him that Mohan finally had to walk her home. If he would not, then the whole concept of devotion would prove to be false, trust of the devotee will stand nullified. Meera erased her identity to keep Mohan alive, now he too had some responsibility.

It was now the time for *Mahasamadhi*, after all the wandering, pain, suffering, joy and love that was dedicated to Mohan. Meera might have pleaded, "Oh lord!! Either take me to you or come with me to me."

That, probably, was a moment when devotee becomes a God. It is said, Meera was never found again. Meera merged into the idol of Krishna. Eventually, the devotees are absorbed in God.

This was Meera's marriage to Krishna. The mist that had become pleasant, fearless, soaked in colours of love.

With similar dedication, Muhammad Sahib too must have discovered, and composed his duties for him, the duties were his marital knot. His love and devotion were all for duty, *karm* and on the same path of duties he lost everything, yet he found it all.

He would not have thought of becoming the Messiah, but the point was that love only descended when the verses and wisdom rose, and this love also further guided to the path of duties and responsibilities.

Is it not a wonderful journey for Meera's Muhammed? On one side love continued to grow and love itself became *karma*, on the other, *karma* transcended into love. What else can be more beautiful than this amalgamation?

When Amir Khusro says, "*Main Nizam se Naina Mila Aaye re*" (When my eyes met with the eyes of HIM). Hazrat Khusro is also talking about similar bliss here. A connection where two were never required.

The bond that Amir Khusro mentioned here was that of a Guru and a disciple, but it was again a bond of love and devotion. As soon as Khusro saw Hazrat Nizam, he forgot himself. And he mentions that what else is left to see when I have already seen the epitome of beauty? Glimpse of Auliya Nizam immerses in his eyes like it happened for Meera on seeing idol of Mohan.

Hazrat Nizam was a prophet walking the path of Hazrat Muhammad Sahib who brought Islam to new heights through love. A stream of same love again.

The lovers of Nabi

Ahilya in every era

Once again, we are not talking of any religion or beliefs related to it.

This is about experiences, feelings, and emotions -- of connectedness and separation.

The saga of Shri Ram's life is quite popular and despite being Hindu Mythology, people around the world are aware of it. There are numerous research papers written on The Ramayana.

There were many people who came in contact with lord Rama, however, all the researches are around few characters and others have been forgotten.

Has anyone ever thought of Ahilya or tried to understand her relevance in Ramayana?

If we ask anyone, who from the Ramayana has had the most significant impact on their life, most would answer either Hanuman, Lakshman, or Sita.

However, Ahilya's was the journey of complete transformation in the presence of Rama.

Ahilya is briefly mentioned in the saga of Ramayana. Naturally it is the saga of Lord Ram, therefore, he is the centre of the story. All incidents are centred on him. Lord Rama, once his task with Ahilya was done, moves on to further journey.

Ahilya's association with Shri Rama is so brief that, perhaps, many of us will not even remember her.

After *Sitaharan* (Sita's abduction by Ravana), when Shri Ram and Lakshman were frantically searching for her in the forest. In the process, both passed through Gautama Rishi's hut. Near his hut, there was a big rock and Ram's feet touch the rock by chance and surprisingly the rock transfigures into a woman, in the form of Ahilya.

Ahilya was a beautiful woman. It is also a strange miracle that Ahilya was not born, she was created by Brahma and then Ahilya was gifted to Gautam Rishi. Ahilya, since beginning, probably was supposed to be abandoned only.

We are talking about this because it is possible that we may not remember this reference, maybe we are not aware only.

How was it possible for a human to transform into a rock?

This stone was just an impression of the way generally a human lives. Every person is probably living a monolithic, a rock like life in one way or the other.

We have different reasons. But the fact is that everyone, at some time or the other, feel rock like heaviness in our heart as we keep on adjusting or compromising mostly.

Sometimes circumstances in life, sometimes responsibilities and sometimes events happen such that we become like rocks while breathing, while walking, however we are not even aware of it.

We are mostly unable to hear our own voice, and recognise our own emotions and feelings.

Then Shri Ram arrives. His touch frees Ahilya from all her burdens. Living under the burden, accepting what came across, she might have had forgotten her own worth, her choices and her happiness.

Ram touched her, the pure and serene love that could instil confidence and self-admiration which allowed her to live again instead of surviving only. Rama liberated her.

Acceptance is Salvation however; acceptance of this truth is equally important.

The story is such that Lord Indra disguises as Gautama Rishi and tries to be intimate with Ahilya. That very moment the Rishi comes back to find his wife with Indradev who of course had trapped Ahilya by disguising as Rishi. The sage gets very angry at his wife. His anger was for a reason that why Ahilya could not recognise Indra and he curses her for betrayal. Ahilya converts into a huge piece of rock and loses her identity.

Ahilya's love and dedication towards her husband was such that despite being a deity, Indradev, had to disguise as Gautama Rishi to subdue her. But that probably was not of much importance for the sage, rather strange.

That is why man is said to be superior that he always carries his personal responsibilities and tasks, or at least tries to, no matters what the situations are. Rock-turned Ahilya waited for years and then that was her *karma*. A woman can accomplish completion only when she has Shri Ram i.e. total love to hold her and stand by her. Love that is serene, gentle, but firm. A woman spends her entire life waiting for a moment that prepares her for this liberation and for acceptance. Once she has it, then she easily surrenders herself to that incomparable love.

But is this only about the woman?

Have we ever tried to understand the life of Hazrat Muhammad carefully?

If not, we can try now. While performing his duties, we understand that responsibility, determination, perseverance and hardship completed the life of Hazrat Muhammad. On the other hand, the same attributes make him a rock also. War, sacrifice, accusations and all this along with the spiritual journey would not have been easy.

The liberation that Ahilya had after the arrival of Shri Ram was important and the same growth happened to the Prophet eventually while he was performing his duties.

On the one hand, Mighty Hazrat Muhammad , who fought innumerable wars throughout the life with the chieftains of the tribes, on the other hand, Hazrat Muhammad was also the source of lifelike energy for everyone involved in those battles. Life like a flowing waterfall amidst the mountain ranges.

There was also a danger in Ahilya's transformation. When the feet of Shri Rama must have hit the rock, Ahilya, Lakshmana must have planned to destroy the rock. Poor thing what would he do also? He too was so much in love with his brother, Lord Rama that he could destroy anyone attempting to harm Rama.

Lakshman had left everything behind and chose to stay and serve his brother Sri Rama. Whereas, for Ahilya just a touch of his feet was enough for her.

Who knows whether Ram will arrive for our liberation or we have to take the responsibilities on our own like Meera?

Meera must also have experienced the uninteresting, indifferent heavy rock inside her many times in the journey of surrender. Till the time she might have not found her Mohan in her inner heart, we do not know how many wounds would be caused by her inner stone?

Krishna must have realised this too, leaving his Vrindavan while offering his flute to Radha.

Whether it is of Shri Rama, of Krishna, of Muhammad or of Meera, Ahilya is alive at all the time. Sri Rama may not be able to reach everywhere, but we are all capable, like Meera and Hazrat Muhammad , to find our own Rama. Just a little faith and a little patience, and we have to keep moving.

In this context, here are a few lines of a beautiful song sung by Manna Dey.

जीवन कहीं भी ठहरता नहीं है

आँधी से, तूफ़ाँ से डरता नहीं है

तू ना चलेगा तो चल देगी राहें

ओ... तू ना चलेगा तो चल देगी राहें

मंज़िल को तरसेंगी तेरी निगाहें

तुझको चलना होगा, तुझको चलना होगा.....

No matters what, we have to keep moving on, keeping your eyes on the destination. May come the storm, we cannot stop...

..... ***Life does not stop anywhere, storms do not frighten it, if you do not walk then paths will walk, Oh! If you do not walk then paths will walk, your eyes will pine for your destination, you will have to walk, you will have to walk...***

It is a strange situation for Ahilya, sometimes she is considered as a great woman to abide by her husband's orders, easy acceptance of curses. Sometimes guilty of betrayal to her husband. It is complicated to understand love. In any case, even Ahilya was completely in control of love, love for her husband. Else if sage Gautama was husband only, practicing his rights of a husband will not give him enough power to curse his wife. Ahilya would not undergo this if Ahilya would not accept her husband's curse with love and dignity?

Ahilya being rock is still understandable, the rock turning into Ahilya is of more importance in a human's life.

The stone too might have learnt patience when it embraced the art of waiting. So, it is understandable, that there certainly is a possibility of this awakening for living man.

Both Meera and Hazrat Muhammad understood the value of this patience.

Hazrat Muhammad believed only on the immense power, which always remained with him, in form of that third one, but patience was also necessary here.

Hazrat Muhammad once meditated in the cave of Mount Hira, he saw the Angel Jibrael. He had brought the first message to Hazrat Muhammad of that third, the invisible one. After that, Hazrat Muhammad kept trying for three years, but had only despair. For once he even felt that it was all an illusion.

One day again he received another message like this from the Angel and in this way it took him twenty three years to understand this whole process.

Meera always believed in the absence of that third one of Hazrat Muhammad which he referred to with Abu Bakar in the cave while hiding.

She always danced to his presence within her and kept saying....

Na Peer na hari

Bas main aur meri hi meri

The responsibility is ours, no one else can help us with it

So, is it possible that Sri Rama comes for every rock-shaped Ahilya? Perhaps, that's why texts like Gita and Quran would have been written so that guidance would continue.

Like every stone that has the potential to become Ahilya, Meera's life was an example to the same and she liberated herself in the process.

Couplets of Rumi-Poetries of Meera

Sufi Mystic Rumi taught us how love and devotion complement each other and the ultimate destination is surrendering to the beloved.

Here is a short story.

There was a man who was wandering around in search of God and he finally reaches to his destination. He arrives to the address that was said to be home of God. He knocks on the door loudly. An equally loud voice comes from inside.

"Who is it?"

The man says, "It is me."

Again, he heard from inside, "There is no room for two people here. You can go back".

The man goes away, seeking. In the same disorientation, he keeps on wandering and searching for God. Years later, he once again reaches at the same door.

He knocks the door again and hears the same voice and the same question from inside, "Who's there?"

The man says, "It is you, in me as well, I am you." The door opens for him and closes as soon as he enters the house of God.

Rumi says, the distance between God and us is just as much as of the mind and heart. On that day, this wanderer ended that gap and found his seeking.

Keeping religions and times aside, if we try to study Rumi and his talks about love -- The Pritam -- we will find it similar to Meera's expression of devotion and love in every way.

After all, love is love and the lovers are lovers, other than similarities what else would they have? Rumi and Meera are all about the love that reaches to the highest level of devotion and oneness.

Where Meera's wandering finally dissolved in her beloved, keeping the lord within her, Rumi said that we were always one, there are no two. It is also a coincidence.

The gap of centuries, between 1,200 and 1,500 BC was erased by one similarity between Meera and Rumi, their ability to Love, the heights and depths of consciousness. Meera may have never even heard of Rumi, and for Rumi, of course it was impossible, the difference between their physical existences was almost of 300 years.

Afghanistan-born Jalaluddin Rumi was steeped in love of God whom he considered to be his Beloved.

His devotional poems lately have become very popular in India. All his writing is in Persian or Arabic script. Meera of course never came across them. But where was the need only for her to study love? She was born full of it. Love is free from the boundaries of language in every age, every time. There is no technique to be learned from each other.

Later conferred with the title of Sufi Saint, Jalaludin Rumi was a teacher, but his search was such as if it continued since centuries. He chose to ramble from Afghanistan to Turkey and Persia.

All these areas are covered with desert which is again another similarity between the two, Rumi and Meera.

Once upon a time, while Rumi was passing through a desert, he saw some children playing in the desert village.

They were revolving in circular formation making rounds and laughing loudly when they stopped, the looked in merriment.

Rumi tried to rove in the same way, copying them and realised that it was such a feeling of joy as if God himself came and joined them in this game!

What else does one want? A loving heart like of him when have met their lover. And then Rumi said;

"Beloved and lover never meet anywhere,

They live in each other"

It is a wonderful coincidence between Meera and Rumi. It feels as if they were talking about each other.

This fun game is a discovery of Rumi, which we call Whirling, and the result of this whirling is cheerfulness. This same whirl was probably the dance of Meera for her beloved that she performed in the widespread desert putting on her anklet.

Maybe Rumi's verses later on were recognized as the songs of love and pain that Meera sang waiting for her beloved's glimpses.

Who would have understood Meera's Mohan if the desert did not stand as a silent witness to these songs and verses?

Rumi attaches so much importance to this whirling that he says;

"Dance when you are broken open,

Dance if you've torn the bandage off,

Dance in the middle of the fighting.

Dance in your blood. Dance when you are perfectly free."

When Maulana Rumi whirled continuously for thirty-six hours, he realised that our centre remains stable no matter how much we move. A tornado arises or a thunderstorm comes, the centre remains unmoved.

This centre is where the home of the beloved is. The one he is looking for outside is within that stable centre, within us. And to meet him one just needs to meet himself.

And the way to meet God is this dance, which Meera also comprehended as she spent her life singing, swinging and playing her *ikatara* (a small Indian musical instrument with one string).

Devoting himself in love and in his verses, Sufi Fakir Rumi taught everyone a lesson from music to silence Sumiran-Remembrance. Rumi says;

"Only silence is an expression of God - love."

Sufi Fakir Rumi introduced the Suf to the world but even today, that Suf is being divided in religions.

Why only Rumi? Meera also was a Sufi, so was Krishna as well as Jesus. Wherever, as far as love spreads, there is an impression of the Sufi. Suf is nothing other than approach of living in complete surrender, total submission to the divine, to the beloved.

But, do people divided in religions, understand this esoteric secret?

By sacrificing love in this division of religion, we are denying the truest approach of life.

As a witness to this massacre, a Sufi dies again and again, and all religions die as soon as love vanishes. That is why eventually religions are becoming dead religions.

Suf is the approach of worship, of a total love. Here no fear of losing or charm of benefits survive. Sufism is all about releasing self at the first place.

A drop of tear that a person offers on the feet of his beloved, this moisture in his eyes is all that he has and when he dances in ecstasy; that is the only way of celebration for him.

Beyond logic and reasons when devotion happens it is the Suf and all those who were searching for themselves in search of their beloved are Sufi. Was Meera not the same? One who found her Mohan in herself and she vanished in him, in cosmic oneness.

Although, many consider Sufi to be a part of Islam, however, what does a Sufi have to do with Islam?

Sufi is simply an approach connecting spirit to spirit, soul to soul. The path that removes the otherness between the devotee and God. Now to celebrate the custom of no anger, no jealousy only celebration of life. Just the ocean of love, in which as deep we drown, as much we emerge, and then the ocean becomes our own.

There is no other transaction. Sufi was always prevalent, before Mohan, before Muhammad even before Meera. Maybe unknown, undiscovered but it was there.

If someone had understood Meera, we would have known that she too was a prophet. We were so busy dividing religions that we could not see her drowning in love and becoming one with her beloved.

As Maulana Rumi says:

"This is Love:

To fly towards a secret sky

To cause a hundred veils

To fall each moment.

First to let go of life

Finally, to take a step without feet"

A Sufi is the one who is thankful for not only what he has, but also, for what he does not have. So was Jallaludin Rumi and so was Meera.

When the heart starts burning, it smells like INCENSE- Rumi.

Meera- Beginning or an End

Beginning or the end, what will happen first? It seems that if somethings start then only will it end. But in the same way, the beginning will be possible only when something ends.

And nothing like this starts or ends, this is just a series, which goes on. Although things keep going in their own rhythm, as per the set pattern; we find them happening differently.

Firstly, we could not understand death, acceptance of death is a distant thing.

Actually, to know life we need to start from knowing death first. But life itself is so mysterious that it has been covered under countless sheets and layers. Who has come to know it yet?

Acceptance of Death is an art that comes out of fearlessness. When we become independent and live life without worrying about the end. Life can be rejoiced possibly only when death is accepted.

As truly stated by many philosophers, we live to the fullest if we are aware that we are not going to have life forever. But what comes first, what to accept first? No one knows.

Meera accepted death in the form of love for Mohan or we can say that love also is a form of death, however, an accomplished one.

How can love be an accomplished death?

We have an answer to this how. Love is the only force that liberates, frees from anger, ego, and jealousy. Love not only connects with the other, in fact love connects us more with our self.

Once in love, we no more are the same, the older one dies and comes alive an improved, dedicated, compassionate and surrendered version of us.

Death is not about end of breath, death is about triumph of consciousness which is achieved through compassion and the seeds to it are love.

A life that stops breathing does not really die. Meera knew that it just was a time to part ways with the world.

Death is something that enlivens the lifeless like rocks.

Like Muhammad Sahib lived, never stopped, and never tired. He kept teaching us dedication, duty, acceptance, and sacrifice. Compassionate similarly as Meera lived an example in her life.

Whatever in life we achieve, that achievement is a result of acceptance and with each acceptance happens one death and a new life.

The moment we surrender ourselves to the lord or to the

beloved, now the one who was there earlier, struggling to make this submission is dead. There was a different way of living just a moment back and now it is different.

Dancing in deserts singing, "*Shyam mane Chakar rakho ji*- Shyam allow me your service", that day Meera died and was born again. The new Meera was the one who was devoted to her Mohan and only desire she had was to dissolve in Mohan, to discover her true self.

Her death and reincarnation brought her to the infinite heights of love. And in those heights whom did she find? Oneself!

Losing yourself and meeting yourself is a wonderful coincidence. Isn't it?

Repeatedly accepting death after death, Meera could still walk on her path of devotion.

When Meera would have picked up the bowl of poison in her hand, did she think of the next moment?

It is said that Meera went on consuming the poison like a sacrament and left singing in her joy. Meera knew that she belonged to Mohan. Now it was his wish that she blossoms like lotus in marsh or flows like sand in desert. It was not Meera's responsibility anymore to think because she had surrendered herself, she had already chosen death and this death gave her the right to love. Meera is immortal, she was called a saint.

Does this happen to us, feeling dead despite being alive? Despite breathing, is it necessary that we are living?

That day while gulping poison, Meera really eradicated herself and raised her love and beloved to the highest stature. In that devotion was such strength that it transformed poison into nectar. That bowl of poison became a symbol of acceptance.

Now there was no sorrow no pain, it was only joy. Rejoicing her Mohan, how Meera dances insanely.

Death is a celebration for those who die conscious, and here Meera also had the right to choose her death.

As Meera eliminated the being of two, now there was no fear of losing beloved due to death. No pain of separation had any existence as Meera had her beloved within her, so for Meera non-presence of Mohan was more significant; more sacred.

Muhammad Sahib did not have to drink the bowl of poison, but in every sip of life, he was served with poison. Sometimes as a challenge, sometimes as expectation, sometimes as a responsibility, and each time he lived adopting death which made him immortal. Meera had love, Muhammad Sahib had duties, but both had their actions fixed, *karma* predecided. And, both continued on their path fearlessly.

Mohan's Meera became immortal, accepting both love and death until she reaches to Meera's Meera, through Hazrat Muhammad .

Poison or Nectar?

Not everyone who consumes poison is Shiva, nor does the cup of every poison becomes nectar.

We have spoken many a times about Meera consuming a bowl of poison, actually her entire life was such that it seemed she was always served with one. However, now why are we discussing the poison of Shiva?

Is this not the churning happening? Our inner churning, so when its churning, we may get a basket containing a snake that turns out to be flowers and at the same time a vessel full of poison to be held by Shiva in his throat.

However, here we are going to talk of celebration and joy. Rejoicing in the name of lord, drowning in him even the poison becomes nectar.

In this whole churning of Meera's Muhammad, there is only one transcript - 'Discover yourself'.

Love and devotion can be for anyone and everyone, however, if we remain unaware of ourselves, then it is nothing more than living a purposeless life.

There will be no difference whether the bowl has poison or nectar because it is us who can eliminate the difference.

Both Shiva and Meera can be called complete in themselves. Those who proclaim immortality in poison.

The greatest lovers and illustrators of hermitage. Shiva immersed and meditated in his own cognizance. The same state of meditation was devotion for Meera.

Shiva performed the Tandava in Virah, pain of separation with his beloved and the same Tandava also became a symbol of Shiva's wrath.

Shiva's solitude happened to be Meera's state of devotion. There was no need for any other.

On the journey of self-discovery, Meera was not searching for anyone else. There is no similarity between Meera and Shiva, but they are still same, what is the difference?

When Meera drank the poison, she drank with the belief that the one who is seated in her conscience as Mohan, can never die.

If we can see carefully, then we will know that whatever is happening in our life, we are the centre of it. All the nectars and poisons rest in us in the form of various emotions and greed.

Any knowledge or preaching is of no use to us until we have tasted the poison and nectar within us.

Meera had tasted such a nectar in her heart that the poison had been neutralised thereafter. Most important and difficult task is to uncover our own layers and dive within ourselves.

The poison Meera consumed, was abandoned by Shiva a long ago by holding it in his throat. Either way, both had tasted their nectar first to devour the poison.

Shiva held the poison to save the universe; else with him, it was the end of all. Meera consumed it because she knew it was her lord's wish who sat inside her.

Both were still alive after consuming poison as they were already accomplished in their own ways. They were complete, death had nothing to take away as they were the beginning and end. The taste of poison was different because of their karmas. On the one hand, Shiva's karma was that of a protector and Meera's was that of surrender and faith.

Both had different responsibilities.

Shiva has many admirers. These admirers carry pride in being Shiva's celebrants since Shiva is a symbol of courage and renunciation. Meera does not have any followers, however, the fact is whether it is courage, renunciation, surrender, or faith, understanding these qualities is not easy. But Meera decoded them all.

We have always heard that Shiva was the first meditator. What is the meaning of Shiva's meditation? The emptiness of thought, expectation, imagination. Meera attained the same emptiness with love, and drowning in love.

In the state of devotion that Shiva lived in meditativeness, in the same state Meera lived in love.

But the venom given to both could not inflict death on them

because they were beyond the process of beginning and end.

Shiva has the whole world. If Shiva had consumed the poison, the whole creation could have been endangered, but he held the poison in his throat and protected the creation. And on the other hand, Meera, who consumed poison, showed the possibility of such dedication that poison can also be made nectar. So, here the taste of Meera and Shiva's venom were different.

Whether it is courage or surrender, it is very difficult to accept both because it is the first to boycott, as in drop the 'I' and then accept come what may.

Have we ever seen Nataraja, the state of dance, Shiva's dance, which is the best method of meditation? Dance takes us to the ultimate state that connects us with all our innermost feelings, with our inner consciousness. Meera unified her emotions by remaining connected to the same consciousness and lived in nothingness.

Neither are we courageous enough to hold the poison, nor lovers who drink the poison.

Courage has a great importance in Islam. From the very beginning, sacrifices were pillars of Islam. Hassan and Husayn the lineage of Hazrat Muhammad, his grandsons who bowed their heads to God, and they sacrificed themselves happily on the path of duty. How can one forget the battle of Karbala and sacrifice of Husayn at that adolescent age?

How would it be easy to forget yourself, erase yourself and yet keep yourself alive?

One can stand just like the Aravalli Mountain, obeying *God's* will. Now, whether the sand dunes continue to rise or the showers of rain are bestowed. This requires a lot of patience and determination. Same like Hazrat Muhammad , he stood, adamant.

In your feet is my heart, Oh beloved, what shall I write

Oh lord, what shall I write?

No words I have, nor wisdom

An unremitting stream, of exiled river,

Whose origin is aim-less,

So is the flow, and timeless deferral

Waiting since ages with one desire,

The one who is the saviour of universe

Will not that lord show me a way?

I am none, you are whole,

This is a feeble bond,

In you only is my home...

Unparalleled similarities

It is all about the omnipresent; the forever consciousness. It is beyond time, era and, of course, religion. When the God is one, Soul is one and consciousness is one, undoubtedly Mohan, Muhammad and Meera too were always present. Meera had to be present as she is not a person, not an identity. She is a state of being for each one who has lived till date.

The Holy Quran was integrated years after the death of Hazrat Muhammad . The purpose was to immortalise the teachings and messages of the Prophet for dispersal of generations for ages. To make the divine messages eternal.

And why not? All that was timeless, so it was important to making an attempt to bring it to the people.

Whether teachings of the Gita or the verses from the Quran, the message that is most important in these both is karma (duties) and love-compassion.

Both the scriptures mention that God is one, formless shapeless, invisible but eternal. The Truth is God.

Krishna's teachings in Kurukshetra, in the middle of war, known as Mahabharat was later identified as Bhagvad Gita. So, whether it is Gita or verses of the Holy Quran of Hazrat Muhammad , they say that the saviour will incarnate. May be a lord, maybe prophet, but the power will arrive to align the world and set a balance again to eliminate turbulence whenever there will be any kind of destruction to the mankind.

Hence the Gita and the Quran agree with each other that the saviour is there.

However, there is a slight difference. Hinduism says that there is a difference between the Prophets i.e. messenger and a deity and hence, Krishna was not a messenger. Mohan was God himself. Hazrat Muhammad and Jesus Christ, were messengers because they received God's command or message and interpreted them in their own way and explained it to the people.

No matter what, the fact is that the saviour is there and when nature requires balance and humans fail to provide, then someone else does it.

Are we all not a part of God, a creator? We all are bestowed with the qualities of becoming a God. The qualities are already mentioned in the previous chapters and one very important reminder is -- have we all not discussed that we are in the process of discovering our inner God, being God.

Mohan explained the rights and wrongs to the world. He says, if we need to fight even our own ones, we should for righteousness, or *dharma*. He also taught about patience and deeds. So did the Prophet. Sometimes, does it not look like Mohan and Hazrat Muhammad are talking about the same realities? In fact, most of the time. Fighting numerous battles with Quraysh, whereas he himself was one of the same tribe.

There are many similarities between Hazart Muhammad and Mohan.

Both had to live with others, away from their parents. Mohan and Hazrat Muhammad were separated from their parents at birth and were raised by the other people.

Both were shepherds in their childhood. If Mohan used to graze cows, Hazrat Muhammad , sheep and goats. It is said that both were very beautiful. We have been aware of the description of Mohan's beauty. Although, not much has been said about the form of Hazrat Muhammad , but we have also heard that he too was the epitome of beauty.

Both had to leave their birthplace and workplace, for some reason or the other. Mohan was born in a jail in Mathura. From there he was transported towards Vrindavan, for his protection as he was in danger since birth. After growing up in Vrindavan, he had to leave again everything behind and kept moving forward on the path of duty to Mathura for Kamsa's end.

Muhammad Sahib also lived this emptiness from the very beginning. Childhood was spent in a group of nomads. Then even when he came back home, Mecca-born Hazrat Muhammad had to spend his life in Medina and had to fight many wars to return home and the movement continued to many other places. Both of them happened to be witnesses to the deaths of many loved ones one after the other during their lifetime. So much pain to bear.

Both left the prophecy of monotheism.

Both shared love and compassion, but had to fight a war on their paths of duty. Sometimes with weapons and sometimes with wisdom. Both were calm and simple by nature, affectionate and empathetic.

One common message in Gita and Quran is about war. War for right, war for the benefit of mankind and war in favour of justice. Gita talks of *Dharma Yuddha* and Quran of *Jihad*, but in none is there any mention of religion.

Here it was more about *karmas* - duties rather than religion. Both the Gita and the Holy Quran are about surrender and faith.

While Radha Krishna's love is beyond examples, it is also said that the love between Hazrat Muhammad and his wife Khadija was also not seen anywhere before. Hearts full of love and the most powerful ones who could surrender themselves to the serenity of Love keeping its virtue as prime.

In spite of it, Krishna had to leave behind Radha and this is also said that he married many women to protect them, giving them shelter so that there would be no persecution in the subject henceforth against them. Hazrat Muhammad had 13 wives for the same reason -- to protect the honour of women after the wars. And sometimes to strengthen the ties between tribes, in order to form a strong and powerful union, to spread Islam.

Strangely, whether it was about Mohan or Hazrat Muhammad, woman who is the source of energy, strength and power, had to be protected by others.

Meera was the only one who could take a stand, only she could rebel all alone. She was probably aware that she had nothing to lose.

Both Mohan and Hazrat Muhammad faced stigmas, sometimes for deceiving and sometimes for being harsh. Mohan conspired against the army of the Kauravas, for the victory of *Satya* – or the Truth. On the other hand, Hazrat Muhammad took many steps to win the war, which he may not have liked personally, but those were the need of the time.

So if we see, both Mohan and Hazrat Muhammad , while walking on the path of *karma*, performed and undertook tasks which might have been seemingly unacceptable. However, those actions are understandable as they were the need of the time.

Now let's talk about Meera. What did she have to do to get into all this mess? Her deeds and religion all were love.

She neither had to prove anything nor did she have to fight any war. There was not even scope of any internal battle as she was always aware of her Mohan.

By accepting God as her own, Meera had learned a great deal from both the knowledge of the Gita and the Quranic teachings.

Mohan and Muhammad did not have much fanfare during their lifetime, although today there are many who chant their names.

But the most notable similarity between all three is that they were all misunderstood. We could not understand Mohan and Hazrat Muhammad and we are still confused as we carry out the devotion of Meera for love for Mohan instead of her self-search.

Meera-*hood*, The Metaphor

Shri Rama along with his brother Shri Lakshman while wandering in the forest in search of his abducted wife Sita reach a place in the forest where Shabri lived.

Shabri was an old lady who had spent her whole life waiting for Shri Ram to visit her place.

Her belief in Shri Ram was strong, unwavering. She knew Ram would come one day. Then she would have the joy of seeing the one she had been, probably, waiting for ages. The protracted waiting for Shri Ram kept adding to her patience and logic as she grew older.

Shabri was a devotee who is said to be an icon of patience and reverence.

In her devotion for Shri Ram, Shabri often preserved some fruits for him. The heights of her innocence and trust in Shri Rama enabled her to taste the berries that fell from the trees. She saved the sweet ones for the lord and threw away the bitter ones.

Now this pure devotee did not bother to think that tasted fruits are considered impure to offer to the lord. She just wanted to serve with the best that she could to the one she had been waiting for since ages.

This *darshan* (seeing) of Shri Ram was much a necessity for Shabri's attainment or *Mahasamadhi* (*the act of consciously and intentionally leaving one's body at the time of death*.)

Patience and devotion change the flow of rivers and move the mountains. So, how could the lord not be moved to hear Shabri's prayers?

Perhaps, the purpose of the lord's arrival was Shabri's attainment.

Eating those delicious berries with joy, Shri Rama asks Shabri whether she had seen Sita somewhere around?

Shabri smiles and replies, "Lord, if you found me, you will certainly find Sita. You had not ever seen me, and yet, you found me. When did Mata Sita part away from you?"

Shri Ram bows down in humility, witnessing Shabri's honesty.

After all, virtues like faith and patience hold utmost importance. Ahilya, the rock full of reverence, also waited for long with the same virtue like of Shabri.

Hazrat Muhammad rejected idol worship years ago in favour and acceptance of the formless God. Whereas, the same Mohan's idol, Meera saved in her heart as her foundation, accepting the non-presence of the lord.

This foundation was not necessary for Mohan's existence. There was no need for any such proof, however, Meera needed this foundation. She resurrected the one formless which was erased by Hazrat Muhammad. Devotion that begins through love ultimately reaches to its perseverance and, subsequently, to surrender.

So, ultimately, Meera required this foundation to start her journey of self-discovery that needed lots of confidence in the self. This confidence needed a source. Mohan was that source for Meera.

Although, we may feel that where was the need to deny or accept the idol? Did Hazrat Muhammad really need to refute idol worship?

Maybe not, however, sometimes it is important to ignore such references. If Hazart Muhammad had not disproved idols, then probably, till date we would have been searching for God in various idols instead of recognising our own potentials and ability to be the one.

Even if we have numerous idols as Gods, they will remain to the namesake. The journey, ultimately, is ours and we should discover it ourselves. Meera's dedication was such that the formless kept on making way for his dispersal to her and Meera was wrapped by her Mohan, her consciousness always in her path full of difficulties.

The same surrender led to an extreme conscience due to which Khwaja Moinuddin Chishti's sitar itself began to play melodious music, when he did not even touch it.

It is said that Khwaja Moinuddin Chishti loved music and practiced for hours. Once, Hazrat Abdul Kadar Jilani came to meet Khwaja Chishti. Since Islam forbids musical pursuits, Khwaja was unable to perform riyaz (*practice*) in the presence of Hazrat Abdul Kader Jilani. He hid his sitar so that Hazrat Jilani does not feel dishonoured. It was time for riyaz and when Khwaja did not arrive for practice, the entire palace came alive with music. Finally, Hazrat Abdul Kader Jilani had to allow Khwaja to continue with his music practice.

After all, how can Suf be separated from music?

So, music is the bond of liberation, the fusion of rhythm, like an amalgamation of souls. The strings that started playing music on their own is an example that music connects with the soul. Such as the incorporation of the Sufi to music.

The authority that we achieve through the spirit of love and dedication, that precisely remains no more in an authority. It is an accomplishment of love that happens after complete surrender to the lord, to the beloved. This authority or this accomplishment stays with us till the time we are alive. Now in that love Hazrat Muhammad erased all the names and, Meera, on the other hand, immersed in the names. Ultimately, it was their individual way to reach to the self through the formless, nameless or shapeless forms.

We may say....

Being God is discovering the self,

Only then will God be with God within us.

Shri Ram would not have come to kill Ravana. That would not be the purpose of his visit. Ravana had the blessing of death by his choice. Ravana had chosen this for himself, an attainment through Shri Rama. Shri Ram must have arrived at Ahilya's site, moved by her patience. Similarly, Shabri's faith must have pulled Shri Ram in the abundance of love.

Was the preaching of the Gita important for Mohan? If he wished, why would there be the war of Mahabharata? On his wish, would not every warrior call off the war? Will they not abandon their weapons and armours, mesmerised the moment Mohan played his flute? Where was the need of Gita or even the war?

Hazrat Muhammad too, would not have arrived to make the Holy Quran alone. Neither, the establishing Islam could be an objective for him. All of them had come to explore their inner truth, discover themselves, the state that can be called Meera-***hood.***

To find oneself, to drop the continuous war within them and outside, to find themselves and their own consciousness, to free themselves.

Meera understood this and this is what Meera lived also.

All of them wanted to achieve Meerahood, the state of super consciousness. So, then what happened to Meera? What was Meera supposed to be? Of course, nothing; she was as it is complete. Like conscience and virtue, that survives in each one of us.

We all have this opportunity of freedom. Only our inner consciousness is to be attained. And what else is Meera?

Meera belongs to no one, no Mohan, no Muhammad. Meera is a stage, a state such as love, meditation, life, such as death. Like the true source; like power and silence. The sweetness of syrup to the thirsty stranded in the desert.

Meera is just an opportunity for all of us to have.

All are contained in Meera and Meera is in all.

Meera demonstrated the wisdom and teachings of Mohan and Hazrat Muhammad , combined in her way of living. And, at the same time, she explained that it is possible for everyone to be Meera.

This is the journey of Meera Ke Muhammad, Meera's Muhammad. Conversation of neither a religion nor century nor time.

Just surrender and acceptance, ability and authority, love and faith.

The attainment of nothingness in completion of self-discovery.

"सफ़र तुम्हारा है,
तुम ही तय करो
सफ़र में मंजिलें नहीं,
मुश्किलें आती हैं,
मिलती है ख़ाक..."

Bhavin Shastri-Author

I consider or not,

Believe it or not,

Your volley remains unmatched.

I may not call you a God,

I still have instances of your presence around me.

Bhavin Shastri, who has travelled on his journey with a firm belief in a possibility of being God. He is on a continuous journey of life, music, and spiritual pursuit. He believes that the most precious thing that we get every day as a gift is a thought. It is this thought process that makes us Buddha and Kabir, if we can understand them properly.

Bhavin Shastri is living example of the spiritual revolution and that is why he also encourages others to meet the God within themselves.

He says that it is time to realise our own possibilities and become God. For this, we just need to find the power within us that first makes us human.

"An expedition that leads a human to encounter their true self is the real journey," says the author.

Bhavin Shastri is an eminent artist who through his music spreads the message of love and peace - a person who understands human emotions and lives life like a witness.

He has been awarded the title of 'Shahanshah-E-Sufi' for his magical singing and Sufi lifestyle. But when he is asked about Sufism, he says that Suf is just a spirit, an approach to life. There is no emperor or beggar in this, we are only lovers. Sufi is one whose search ends in the practice of gratitude.

"Art that cannot bring you salvation is a curse. What else is art? Whatever situation or action that starts giving full enjoyment, becomes art."

-Bhavin Shastri

Book *Lockdown-21- Me to Messiah*, is his first literary venture. He is now presenting his ideology as his second book, 'Meera's Muhammad-Meera K Muhammad'.

He is a true patriot. His words and programmes reflect his love and respect for the nation. He has been a major contributor to social development and upliftment of the under privileged. He has adopted the principle of sharing in his life as a virtue. He says "What we have is good enough' and hold an ability of sharing what is extra."

Being an amazing orator, he connects with youth easily. He motivates the next generation to trust themselves.

अजीब सा शहर है तेरे अंदर,

तेरी हुकूमत, तूं ही ग़ुलाम...

Gratitude

First, thanks to the thoughts that we get every day. Perhaps, because of this thought process, life has a purpose.

After that, thanking the breath that enables us to perform our deeds. After all this pandemic could at least teach us the importance of breath.

As long as we are alive, there is a possibility of doing something. After all, *karmas* can be executed only when we are alive.

And then heartiest thanks to conscious conscience that as a witness keeps a watch on our deeds and gives us the ability to decide our right and wrong.

We always fail to thank nature that has arranged so much energy around and has left it all on our dispersal.

Thanks to the sun for the hope and to the evening for smoothening the challenges.

Osho, the philosopher, I owe my transformation to him in many ways.

Every person and situation who has made any contribution in discovering our thoughts by provoking and directing us towards encounters, I, Bhavin Shastri, extend gratitude to all.

Dear Reader,

Everyone who reads this book is requested to first understand that this book does not talk about division based on religions. Here we are talking only about opportunities. After all, the purpose of every religion is spirituality. That is all we are talking about here.

Like Buddhahood is an opportunity for everyone, similarly being a 'Meera' is also a possibility that everyone has.

Just when love happens to be synonymous with life, we became Meera.

We are presenting our thoughts through this book, perhaps, it can be of some use to you.

This book can definitely guide you towards spiritual revolution within you and if that revolution continues there will be numerous opportunities to meet yourself in your own light.

Every reader has the right to agree or disagree with us.

If you want to talk about it after reading the book, please email us @ uchitathakkar5308@gmail.com

Thank you